# PLAYBOY'S BAR GUIDE

## BY THOMAS MARIO

A PLAYBOY PRESS BOOK

# Contents

# Oddballs                                           202

# The Brimming Bowl                                  221

# Hot Cheer                                          233

# Index                                              247

# INTRODUCTION

# Introduction

The number of mixed drinks it's possible to concoct is limited only by the liquor supply and the imagination of the mixer. But in drink making, as in the culinary arts, the best results occur when imagination and creativity are solidly backed by knowledge and experience. Experience comes naturally; supplying the knowledge is the purpose of this guide. In addition to nearly 800 tried and tested drink recipes, we've included suggestions for stocking your bar, a summary of standard bar measurements, tips on creating and serving drinks—glassware, icemanship, mixing, stirring, garnishing, etc.—as well as a drink calculator for large-scale partying.

It's our belief that whenever two or more persons touch glasses, both the liquor and something else begin stirring up fun. That something else is the young appetite for life and for the varied means of enjoying it— PLAYBOY's reason for existence and the reason for this book. Familiarize yourself with the basic tips that follow, consult them for special potables, and every time you pour drinks, you'll generate among your guests the mood described superlatively by Fielding as "one universal grin."

# Stocking the Bar

There are no hard-and-fast rules for stocking a home bar. For the most part, the kinds and quantities of liquor you keep on hand will be determined by your own taste and the preferences of the closely knit group of friends with whom you most regularly share the quiet joys of the cocktail hour. Still, for entertaining casual drop-ins and for spur-of-the-moment soirees, it doesn't hurt to have on hand a basic supply of spirits which will indulge almost any fancy. Since the three standard drinks for satisfying the thirst of 20th Century man are manhattans, martinis and highballs, you can start with the ingredients from which they're made—whiskey, gin and vermouth. One kind of gin will do, but you'll need two kinds of vermouth: sweet and dry. And when it comes to whiskey, you'd do well to stock four kinds: American blended whiskey, bourbon, Scotch and Canadian. In less time than it takes to say daiquiri or screwdriver, you'll realize that rum and vodka would also make worthy additions to your collection. A bottle of each, then, nine in all, are the potables that all barkeepers, public as well as private, constantly reach for, the ones you'd want whether you're host or guest.

# Accessories to Alcohol

Of course, the applied art of mixing drinks also depends on many things that aren't alcohol. Liquor must be made tart, sweet, rich, bitter, foamy and, in countless other ways, congenial to sophisticated taste buds. Frequently it's garnished in a manner that accents a drink's appearance as well as its flavor and aroma, as with the olive in the martini, the cucumber peel in the Pimm's Cup or the strawberry in the champagne cocktail.

Although the total number of accessories available for mixing purposes is far too great to be listed here, there are several which deserve mention simply because they're called for so often. Among them are mixers: bitter lemon, club soda, ginger ale, quinine water, Seven-Up and tomato juice; garnishes, including —but certainly not limited to—cherries, lemons, limes, olives, cocktail onions and oranges; and various additives, such as bitters, sugar, Rose's lime juice and bar foam. Whether or not you should stock other, more exotic bar items will depend on your personal preferences. If, for example, you're turned on by banana daiquiris, you'll obviously need bananas; if your crowd has developed a special fondness for Caribbean rum drinks, you might want to sweeten them with guava jelly melted down to a syrup. And so on. Here, as elsewhere in the barkeeper's art, the question preceding all decisions is, "What do *you* like to drink?"

A couple of points worth remembering when you're laying in supplies are, first, that small containers of seasonings such as bitters are less likely to lose their zest than larger bottles that hang around the shelf too long. Large bottles of syrups such as Falernum will lose their bright color and flavor if untouched for months. If this occurs, don't hesitate to discard the old stock and buy fresh replacements. Second, fruits and other perishables should be emphatically fresh. Whenever possible, use real limes, lemons, orange juice, etc., rather than the bottled, canned or frozen variety.

## Glassware

The glass in which you serve a drink is more than just a medium for transferring liquor from bottle to bibber. It frames the contents for the eye, directs the aroma to the nose and touches the lips before the liquid releases its storehouse of flavor. Small wonder, then, that attractive glasses make drinking all the more pleasurable. You'll find glassware available in two basic shapes: tumbler and stemware. The latter is more gracious to the eye and easier on furniture, since condensation on the cold glass rarely makes its way down to the base. But tumbler glasses are less formal, more secure and usually less expensive. The glasses traditionally used for various kinds of drinks are illustrated here. If you want to limit yourself to two kinds, we suggest the old-fashioned or on-the-rocks glass and the all-purpose tulip-shaped wineglass; with them you'll be able to serve in style anything from ale to zinfandel, champagne to stout.

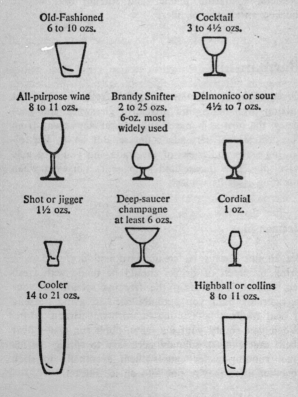

Old-Fashioned
6 to 10 ozs.

Cocktail
3 to 4½ ozs.

All-purpose wine
8 to 11 ozs.

Brandy Snifter
2 to 25 ozs.
6-oz. most
widely used

Delmonico or sour
4½ to 7 ozs.

Shot or jigger
1½ ozs.

Deep-saucer
champagne
at least 6 ozs.

Cordial
1 oz.

Cooler
14 to 21 ozs.

Highball or collins
8 to 11 ozs.

## Tools for the Bar

Bar equipment, like glassware, should be attractive as well as functional. Besides, pleasing eye appeal is frequently a sign of serviceability; what looks good often works well. Among the many gadgets available, the ones any barkeep needs are: a sturdy bottle opener; a double-ended measure, jigger-sized at one end, pony-sized at the other; a corkscrew; measuring spoons and cup; a lemon-lime squeezer; a long-handled barspoon; a mixing-glass-and-shaker set and a coil-rimmed strainer. Other useful items are a cutting board and bar knife; a tray for carrying wet goods from bar to benders; a martini pitcher and stirring rod; an ice bucket; an electric blender.

## Barmanship

Given a choice selection of spirits, fresh and flavorful mixing ingredients and attractive glassware and gadgetry, the host at home is still several steps away from the professional bartender's finesse. But survey the following skills and tricks of the trade and you'll be able to display that finesse and keep your cool even when the fling is at its wildest.

### Icemanship

Ice should always be clean, hard and dry, and each drink or batch of drinks should be made with fresh ice. Hoard your ice in the freezing section of your refrigerator until you actually need it; avoid keeping it near foods, where it may absorb undesirable odors. When you empty your ice trays, don't run water over them unless it's absolutely necessary to spring the ice free; running water causes them eventually to stick together after they're put into an ice bucket.

If you're mixing drinks in a shaker, you'll find that using cubes results in less dilution than either crushed or cracked ice. The ice should always go into the shaker first, alcohol last; by giving ice first place, all the ingredients that follow will be cooled on their way down. When the drinks have been shaken, pour them at once; if extra liquid is left in the shaker, strain it off immediately to prevent its becoming diluted while it waits.

To make crushed or cracked ice for coolers and other tall drinks, use either a manual or an electric ice crusher, or simply wrap cubes in a strong towel or canvas bag designed for this purpose and break them up with a mallet or hammer.

## To Stir or to Shake?

To keep their icy clarity, cocktails made with clear liquors—martinis, manhattans, rob roys, gimlets, etc.— should be stirred, not shaken. For proper dilution, stir every batch of cocktails at least 20 times. But when a carbonated liquid is added to tall drinks, stir very briefly; most of the liquor rises to the top automatically, and excessive stirring only dissipates the sparkle.

Those cocktails calling for eggs, cream, fruit juice, heavy liqueurs or any other hard-to-mix ingredients— such as the alexander, daiquiri, flip, etc.—must be shaken—vigorously!

## Chilling and Frosting Glasses

You can make certain your cocktails are cold by chilling your glasses before filling them. Place them in the refrigerator or freezer until they're cold (ten minutes in the freezer will frost the glass), bury the glasses in cracked ice or fill them with cracked ice and stir the ice a few times before discarding it and pouring the drinks. For a really long-lasting frost, dip the glasses into water and place them in the refrigerator's freezing section for two or three hours.

To sugar-frost a glass, chill it first; then moisten the rim with a wedge of citrus fruit, citrus peel or a liqueur and, finally, dip the moistened rim into a bowl of superfine sugar.

## Fruit Juices and Peels

Always try to use fresh fruit when you're making drinks. Lemons, limes and oranges should be tamed on the cutting board before they're cut for squeezing. With the palm of your hand, lean on the fruit and roll it back and forth a few times, thus softening its flesh so that the juice will flow freely after it's cut. Peels should be cut just before serving to preserve the volatile oils. Use a twist cutter or a very sharp paring knife to shave off only the colored surface of the peel, in 1-by-½-inch sections.

## Simple Syrup

In drinks calling for sugar, some barmen prefer sugar syrup to loose sugar, since it makes drinks velvety smooth and is often easier to use, since it blends without prolonged shaking or stirring. To make it, bring 1 cup of water to a boil and stir in 1 cup of sugar; simmer for 1½ minutes. By that time the mixture will have been reduced to approximately 1 cup, making it possible to substitute equal amounts of syrup for sugar in any bar recipe where it may be preferred.

## Measuring

Guests at a pour-it-yourself bar should feel free to pour as many fingers as they please, but if you, as the host, are preparing any kind of mixed drinks, you should trust the jigger rather than your eye, just as the best professional barmen always do. Even in simple drinks such as Scotch and soda, too much liquor can be unpleasant and, in a way, as inhospitable as too little.

## Bar Measurements

The guide below will provide you with the information needed to plot your way from dash to demijohn. It will also help you take a single drink recipe and magnify it at will or reduce a giant punch-bowl recipe to the desired amount of swig.

DASH—For all drink recipes in this book, a dash means ⅛ teaspoon.

TEASPOON—⅓ tablespoon, or ⅙ ounce.

TABLESPOON—3 teaspoons, or ½ ounce.

PONY—1 ounce.

JIGGER—1½ ounces.

WINEGLASS—As a measuring term, it means 4 ounces.

SPLIT—6½ ounces.

PINT—16 ounces; ½ quart; 2 cups.

FIFTH—25.6 ounces; ⅘ quart; ⅕ gallon.

QUART—32 ounces; 2 pints; 4 cups; ¼ gallon.

HALF GALLON—64 ounces.

MAGNUM—52 ounces; double-size champagne bottle.

JEROBOAM—104 ounces; a little more than 4 fifths. The largest domestic champagne bottle.

TAPPIT-HEN—128 ounces; 1 gallon.

REHOBOAM—156 ounces; about 1⅕ gallons.

METHUSELAH—208 ounces; about 1⅗ gallons. The largest-size champagne bottle exported from France.

SALMANAZAR—312 ounces; about 2½ gallons.

BALTHAZAR—416 ounces; about 3⅓ gallons.

NEBUCHADNEZZAR—520 ounces; slightly more than 4 gallons.

DEMIJOHN—1 to 10 gallons.

# Party Drinking

Party planning sometimes leaves the host in a quandary as to how much liquor he'll need to keep the well from running dry in the middle of the festivities. Recognizing the problem, we've prepared some charts which will tell you at a glance the quantity of spirits required to allay the thirst of from 6 to 30 people. If you're inviting more than 30 guests, you can extrapolate from the charts or, better yet, hire a caterer.

The following guide covers cocktails before dinner or postprandial highballs. If you're serving both, calculate both.

| If you're the host for a party of | As a rule, they'll consume | If drinks are 1½ ozs., you'll need at least | If drinks are 2 ozs., you'll need at least |
|---|---|---|---|
| 6 | 12–18 drinks | 2 fifths | 2 fifths |
| 8 | 16–24 " | 2 " | 2 " |
| 10 | 20–30 " | 2 " | 3 " |
| 12 | 24–36 " | 3 " | 3 " |
| 20 | 40–60 " | 4 " | 5 " |
| 30 | 60–90 " | 6 " | 8 " |

To be on the plus side, quarts may be purchased instead of fifths; often there's a saving in the larger bottles.

Brandy and liqueurs are in a special category when served straight and not as an ingredient in dessert cocktails, liqueur frappés, etc. The usual serving in the small brandy glass as well as the larger brandy snifter is one ounce per person; the same goes for liqueurs served straight.

| When pouring brandy or liqueurs as after-dinner drinks for a party of | As a rule, they'll consume | You'll need the following fifths of brandy or liqueurs |
|---|---|---|
| 6 | 6–12 drinks | 1 fifth |
| 8 | 8–16 " | 1 " |
| 10 | 10–20 " | 1 " |
| 12 | 12–24 " | 1 " |
| 20 | 20–40 " | 2 fifths |
| 30 | 30–60 " | 3 " |

*Note well*: Many small bottles of imported liqueurs are odd sizes such as 23/32 pint or 11.8 fluid ounces. The American fifth is 25.6 ounces. Make adjustments, if necessary, when calculating your party needs.

In estimating carbonated waters such as club soda, tonic water, ginger ale, cola drinks, etc., a generous guideline is to allow a 28-ounce bottle for each two persons.

# COCKTAILS

# Cocktails

The most overwhelmingly popular of all potables, the open sesame to brunch parties, lunch parties, dinner parties, midnight supper parties and the next morning's revival parties, the cocktail is undoubtedly America's most unique contribution to the world of bibulous pleasure. The stories concerning the origin of the word *cocktail* are nearly as many and varied as the mixtures themselves. Among them, the following legends have enjoyed long vintage life:

The word came from the French word *coquetel*, once used to describe a mixed drink in the Bordeaux region; even Frenchmen say *passez-moi* to this one.

Southern army officers were once served a luscious mixed drink by a lovely southern belle. Her name? Octelle, suh!

A distinguished American general was invited to the court of a Mexican monarch whose daughter appeared with a drink in the royal cup of gold encrusted with rubies. When the obvious question of who would drink first racked all the king's men, the daughter solved the problem very intelligently by drinking the libation herself. The stunning princess's name was, of course, Coctel.

Western horse traders whose nags weren't worth the

17

price of their pelts, on sale day, fed their horses liquor whose effects made them cock their tails and come to life with incredible spirits.

Morning tipplers in New Amsterdam, visiting inns for a pick-me-up, would invariably run into Dutch barmaids who (you guessed it) used the tails of roosters for sweeping away last night's litter.

A young Irish lass (this one by James Fenimore Cooper) not only managed to procure and roast chickens from Tory farmers for her Revolutionary guests, but decorated their drinks with feathers from the cocks' tails.

Whether or not these stories are any truer than Bunyan's blue ox, it's clear that the cocktail goes deep into America's drinking heritage. And Americans still remain the foremost masters and idolaters of the cocktail.

Cocktails range from appetite-awakening bone-dry martinis to velvety dessert cocktails that correctly climax a rich feast. Men taking the lead at their own cocktail parties should weigh the counsel in the Introduction under "Barmanship." In time, as your cocktail repertoire expands, the ups and downs of the cocktail shaker will become second nature. But even the most polished perfectionists at their bars follow certain well-tested guidelines for cocktails, hence the following review of the more important considerations in drink making:

1. Inferior liquors aren't masked in cocktails. A fine gin will seem even finer in a martini. The same goes for whiskeys, rums, vodkas and vermouths.

2. Don't imitate free-pouring bartenders in public bars. Use standard measures, whether they be teaspoons, jiggers, ounces, cups or quarts. When you multiply quantities for party drinking, be mathematically accurate.

3. Ice must be hard, cold and clean—not weeping. Fresh ice at zero degrees Fahrenheit or below will produce brisker drinks than ice turning to water.

4. Though cocktails must be icy cold (proper dilution is part of the art), they shouldn't be watery. Anyone can begin shaking cocktails. An artist knows when to stop. Normally 2 to 2¾ ounces poured into a cocktail shaker will grow to 4 to 4½ ounces after proper shaking.

5. Use the proper glass for each cocktail, and be sure that it's sparkling clean and prechilled. The glass should first chill the hand and then the lips; the icy cocktail itself will take care of the rest.

6. You should, of course, use fresh ingredients in your cocktails, especially when it comes to fruit juices.

7. Cocktails with fruit juices, eggs, syrups, etc., are normally shaken; those containing only liquor and vermouth are stirred (although one of the most eminent martini men of modern times, Somerset Maugham, insisted that his martinis be *shaken*). The stirred cocktail is clear; the shaken cloudy.

8. Make your own personal recipe changes only with the greatest care, remembering that some cocktails are dominated by a single, straight, powerful flavor—the martini by gin, for instance, or the negroni by Campari —while others are a medley of flavors: liquors, fortified wines, juices, bitters, fruits, etc. A fine cocktail of the latter type is always in delicate balance; even its aftertaste leaves a pleasant sense of the tart and the sweet, the strong and the weak. Sometimes adding or subtracting an eighth of a teaspoon will make a noticeable difference. Be creative if you will, but create slowly and deftly. A new drink is always an evolution.

The cocktails that follow are designed for a 4½-ounce cocktail glass, except in those cases where an old-fashioned or other glass is used. The parsimonious 3-ounce cocktail glasses are now skeletons in most liquor closets; not only does the larger cocktail provide more sumptuous bliss for the guests, but it's a boon to the host since it means fewer refills and the coveted chance to sit down, drink and enjoy the revels.

# After-Dinner Cocktails

On a dinner or late-supper menu, the after-dinner cocktail can take the place of the dessert or supplement it. As a libation, it's frankly sweet and toothsome. It goes perfectly with a platter of cheese and crackers, a fresh fruit bowl or both. It graciously replaces the ubiquitous pie and the gooey ice cream. For the harried host who has neither the time to make, nor the energy to shop for, a fresh dessert, it's a deliverance. Freshly concocted, any of the following are an imaginative way to conclude a brunch, lunch or dinner.

## BLUE ANGEL

½ oz. blue curaçao
½ oz. parfait amour
½ oz. brandy
½ oz. lemon juice
½ oz. cream

Shake well with ice. Strain into prechilled cocktail glass. Cool, incredibly smooth.

## CADIZ

¾ oz. amontillado
   sherry
¾ oz. blackberry
   liqueur
½ oz. triple sec
½ oz. cream

Shake well with ice. Strain over rocks in prechilled old-fashioned glass.

## CALM VOYAGE

½ oz. Galliano or
   Roiano
½ oz. passion-fruit
   syrup
2 teaspoons lemon
   juice
½ oz. light rum
½ egg white
⅓ cup crushed ice

Put all ingredients into blender. Blend at low speed 10–15 seconds. Pour into prechilled deep-saucer champagne glass. Mendelssohn is good accompaniment on this trip.


## CARA SPOSA

1  oz. coffee liqueur ½ oz. cream
1  oz. curaçao ⅓ cup crushed ice

Put all ingredients into blender. Blend at low speed 10–15 seconds. Pour into prechilled deep-saucer champagne glass. Although any kind of coffee liqueur may be used in this drink, the espresso-coffee liqueur is especially pleasant.


## CHERRY RUM

1¼ ozs. light rum ½ oz. cream
 ¾ oz. cherry liqueur ⅓ cup crushed ice

Put all ingredients into blender. Blend at low speed 10–15 seconds. Pour into prechilled deep-saucer champagne glass.


## CHIQUITA PUNCH

1½ ozs. banana liqueur ¾ oz. grenadine
1½ ozs. orange juice ¾ cup crushed ice
1½ ozs. cream

Put all ingredients into blender. Blend at high speed 10 seconds. Pour into prechilled old-fashioned glass. Created by Bill Nolan, head bartender at the Los Angeles Playboy Club.

## CHOCOLATE RUM

| | |
|---|---|
| *1 oz. light rum* | *½ oz. cream* |
| *½ oz. crème de cacao* | *1 teaspoon 151-proof* |
| *½ oz. crème de menthe* | *rum* |

Shake light rum, crème de cacao, crème de menthe and cream well with ice. Strain into prechilled cocktail glass. Float 151-proof rum on top.

## COFFEE GRASSHOPPER

| | |
|---|---|
| *¾ oz. coffee liqueur* | *¾ oz. cream* |
| *¾ oz. white crème de menthe* | |

Shake well with ice. Strain into prechilled cocktail glass.

## COFFEE ROIANO

| | |
|---|---|
| *1½ ozs. Roiano* | *½ oz. cream* |
| *½ oz. coffee liqueur* | *⅓ cup crushed ice* |

Put all ingredients into blender. Blend at low speed 10–15 seconds. Pour into prechilled deep-saucer champagne glass. May be served not only at the end of a meal but at any time of the day.

## DULCET

| | |
|---|---|
| *1 oz. vodka* | *½ oz. apricot liqueur* |
| *½ oz. curaçao* | *1 teaspoon lemon juice* |
| *½ oz. anisette* | *½ brandied apricot* |

Shake vodka, curaçao, anisette, apricot liqueur and lemon juice well with ice. Strain over cracked ice or rocks in prechilled old-fashioned glass. Add brandied apricot.

## FROZEN BLACK CURRANT

1  oz. crème de cassis    ⅓ cup crushed ice
1  oz. pineapple juice    1 slice orange
½ oz. brandy

Put crème de cassis, pineapple juice, brandy and crushed ice into blender. Blend at low speed 10–15 seconds. Pour into prechilled deep-saucer champagne glass. Add orange slice.

## GOLD CADILLAC

¾ oz. crème de cacao    ¾ oz. cream
¾ oz. Galliano    ⅓ cup crushed ice

Put all ingredients into blender. Blend at low speed 10–15 seconds. Pour into prechilled deep-saucer champagne glass. For another version, omit crushed ice, shake well with ice and strain into prechilled cocktail glass.

## GOLDEN FROG

½ oz. Strega    ½ oz. lemon juice
½ oz. Galliano    ¾ cup crushed ice
½ oz. vodka

Put all ingredients into blender. Blend at high speed 10 seconds. Pour into prechilled old-fashioned glass, as served in the Denver Playboy Club.

## GRASSHOPPER

¾ oz. white crème de    ¾ oz. green crème de
     cacao            menthe
                   ¾ oz. cream

Shake with ice. Strain into prechilled cocktail glass.

## IL MAGNIFICO

¾ oz. Tuaca                ¾ oz. cream
¾ oz. curaçao             ⅓ cup crushed ice

Put all ingredients into blender. Blend at low speed
10–15 seconds. Pour into prechilled deep-saucer champagne glass. Good before, with or after the espresso.

## LIMEY

1  oz. light rum           ⅓ cup crushed ice
1  oz. lime liqueur        1  slice lime
½ oz. triple sec           Lime peel
2  teaspoons lime juice

Put rum, lime liqueur, triple sec, lime juice and crushed
ice into blender. Blend at low speed 10–15 seconds.
Pour into prechilled deep-saucer champagne glass. Add
lime slice. Twist lime peel above drink and drop into
glass. Wonderful dessert cocktail after shish kabob.

## MANGO MINT

1½ ozs. mango nectar       ½ oz. white crème de
1  oz. rum                    menthe
½ oz. cream                ⅓ cup crushed ice

Put all ingredients into blender. Blend at low speed
10–15 seconds. Pour into prechilled old-fashioned glass.
Add a rock or two to fill glass to rim. Delightful to sip
after a lazy brunch.

## MOCHA MINT

¾ oz. coffee liqueur       ¾ oz. crème de cacao
¾ oz. crème de menthe

Shake well with ice. Strain into prechilled sugar-frosted
cocktail glass.

## ORACABESSA

1 oz. banana liqueur
½ oz. lemon juice
½ oz. 151-proof rum

1 slice banana
1 slice lemon

Dip banana slice into lemon juice or orange juice to prevent discoloration. Shake banana liqueur, lemon juice and rum well with ice. Strain over rocks in old-fashioned glass. Add banana and lemon slices.

## ORANGE COMFORT

½ oz. Southern
   Comfort
½ oz. anisette
¾ oz. orange juice

½ oz. lemon juice
1 slice cocktail orange
   in syrup

Shake Southern Comfort, anisette, orange juice and lemon juice well with ice. Strain into prechilled cocktail glass. Garnish with cocktail-orange slice.

## ORANGE FLOWER

1 oz. curaçao
½ oz. cherry liqueur
½ oz. orange juice
1 teaspoon lemon
   juice

1 dash orange-
   flower water
⅓ cup crushed ice

Put all ingredients into blender. Blend at low speed 10–15 seconds. Pour into prechilled deep-saucer champagne glass. Exhilarating finale for a roast-goose dinner.

## PINK ALMOND

½ oz. crème de            1  oz. blended whiskey
    noyaux                ½ oz. kirsch
½ oz. orgeat or           ½ oz. lemon juice
    orzata                1  slice lemon

Shake crème de noyaux, orgeat, whiskey, kirsch and
lemon juice well with ice. Strain over rocks in prechilled old-fashioned glass. Add lemon slice.

## PINK SQUIRREL

1  oz. crème de           1  oz. white crème de
    noyaux                    cacao
                          ¾ oz. cream

Shake well with ice. Strain into prechilled sugar-frosted
cocktail glass. Pinker and smoother than a pink lady.

## RUSSIAN COFFEE

¾ oz. coffee liqueur      ¾ oz. cream
¾ oz. vodka               ⅓ cup crushed ice

Put all ingredients into blender. Blend at low speed 10–
15 seconds. Pour into prechilled deep-saucer champagne
glass.

## SHERRIED COFFEE

1¼ ozs. oloroso sherry    2  teaspoons cream
1¼ ozs. coffee liqueur

Shake sherry and coffee liqueur well with ice. Strain
over rocks in prechilled old-fashioned glass. Float cream
on top.

## SNIFTER

¾ oz. Galliano
¾ oz. brandy
1 teaspoon white
    crème de menthe

⅓ cup finely crushed
    ice

Pour liquors into prechilled brandy snifter. Add crushed ice. Stir. May be served with or without straw. You can get it either way at the Miami Playboy Club.

## SOUTHERN PEACH

1 oz. Southern
    Comfort
1 oz. peach liqueur

½ oz. cream
1 slice fresh or
    brandied peach

Shake Southern Comfort, peach liqueur and cream well with ice. Strain over rocks or coarsely cracked ice in prechilled old-fashioned glass. Add peach slice.

## STRAWBERRY KISS

1 oz. strawberry
    liqueur
½ oz. kirschwasser
½ oz. light rum

½ oz. orange juice
1 teaspoon lemon
    juice
1 large strawberry

Shake strawberry liqueur, kirschwasser, rum, orange juice and lemon juice well with ice. Strain into prechilled sugar-frosted cocktail glass. Add strawberry.

## YELLOW FINGERS

1 oz. gin
1 oz. blackberry
    brandy

½ oz. banana liqueur
½ oz. heavy cream

Shake well with ice. Strain into oversize cocktail glass.

# Aperitifs

## AMERICANO

1¼ ozs. Campari            Lemon peel
1¼ ozs. sweet vermouth     Club soda (optional)

Stir Campari and sweet vermouth well with ice. Strain
into prechilled cocktail glass. Twist lemon peel above
drink and drop into glass. If you prefer, a Delmonico
or old-fashioned glass may be used instead—with a rock
or two and a splash of soda.

## APPLE BYRRH

1  oz. calvados            ½ teaspoon lemon
½ oz. Byrrh                   juice
½ oz. dry vermouth         Lemon peel

Shake calvados, Byrrh, vermouth and lemon juice well
with ice. Strain into prechilled cocktail glass. Twist
lemon peel above drink and drop into glass.

## BITTERSWEET

1¼ ozs. sweet vermouth     1  dash orange bitters
1¼ ozs. dry vermouth          Orange peel
2  dashes Angostura
     bitters

Stir both kinds of vermouth and both kinds of bitters
well with ice. Strain into prechilled cocktail glass. Twist
orange peel above drink and drop into glass.

## BUTTERFLY

¾ oz. dry vermouth         ½ oz. Dubonnet
¾ oz. sweet vermouth       ½ oz. orange juice

Shake everything well with ice. Strain over rocks in
prechilled old-fashioned glass.

## BYRRH BRANDY

¾ oz. Byrrh                    ¾ oz. dry vermouth
¾ oz. cognac

Stir well with ice. Strain into prechilled cocktail glass.


## BYRRH CASSIS

1½ ozs. Byrrh                 1  slice lemon
 ¼ oz. crème de cassis        Iced club soda
 ½ oz. lemon juice               (optional)

Stir Byrrh, crème de cassis and lemon juice well with ice.
Strain over rocks in prechilled old-fashioned glass. Add
lemon slice—and a splash of soda if desired.


## BYRRH COCKTAIL

1¼ ozs. Byrrh                 Lemon peel
1¼ ozs. gin

Stir Byrrh and gin well with ice. Strain into prechilled
cocktail glass or over rocks in prechilled old-fashioned
glass. Twist lemon peel above drink and drop into
glass.


## CALIFORNIAN

1½ ozs. sweet vermouth    2  ozs. orange juice
 1  oz. blended whiskey    1  teaspoon orgeat

Combine and shake well with ice. Strain over large ice
cube in prechilled old-fashioned glass. Be sure the
orange juice is freshly squeezed from ripe California
navels or Valencias in midseason.

## CANADIAN AND CAMPARI

1 oz. Canadian            1  oz. dry vermouth
    whisky                   Lemon peel
½ oz. Campari

Stir whisky, Campari and vermouth well with ice.
Strain into prechilled cocktail glass. Twist lemon peel
above drink and drop into glass. A perfect drink to
sip while anticipating the antipasto.

## CARDINAL II

¾ oz. gin                 ¾  oz. dry vermouth
¾ oz. Campari               Lemon peel

Stir gin, Campari and vermouth well with ice. Strain
into prechilled cocktail glass. Twist lemon peel above
drink and drop into glass.

## COMBO

2½ ozs. dry vermouth      ¼  teaspoon Angostura
½ teaspoon curaçao           bitters
½ teaspoon sugar          1  teaspoon cognac

Shake everything well with ice. Strain over rocks in
prechilled old-fashioned glass. An elusive glow is created
by this combination of aperitif flavors.

## DIABOLO

1½ ozs. imported dry      ¼  teaspoon lemon
    white port               juice
 1  oz. dry vermouth         Lemon peel

Shake port, vermouth and lemon juice well with ice.
Strain into prechilled cocktail glass. Twist lemon peel
above drink and drop into glass.

## DUBONNET COCKTAIL

1¼ ozs. Dubonnet        *Lemon peel*
1¼ ozs. gin

Stir Dubonnet and gin well with ice. Strain into prechilled cocktail glass. Twist lemon peel above drink and drop into glass.


## FINO

1¼ ozs. fino sherry     *1 slice lemon*
1½ ozs. sweet vermouth

Stir sherry and vermouth well with ice. Strain over rocks in prechilled old-fashioned glass. Garnish with lemon slice.


## FLORIDIAN

1½ ozs. dry vermouth    *2 ozs. grapefruit juice*
 ½ oz. Forbidden Fruit   *2 dashes orange bitters*
 1 teaspoon Falernum   *1 slice lime*

Shake vermouth, Forbidden Fruit, Falernum, grapefruit juice and bitters well with ice. Strain over large ice cube in prechilled old-fashioned glass. Garnish with lime slice.


## GIN AND CAMPARI

1¼ ozs. gin        *Orange peel*
1¼ ozs. Campari

Stir gin and Campari well with ice. Strain over rocks in prechilled old-fashioned glass. Twist orange peel above drink and drop into glass. Savor it in sips.

## LILLET COCKTAIL

1½ ozs. Lillet                    *Lemon peel*
1  oz. gin

Stir Lillet and gin well with ice. Strain into prechilled
cocktail glass. Twist lemon peel above drink and drop
into glass.

## LILLET NOYAUX

1½ ozs. Lillet              ¼ teaspoon crème de
1  oz. gin                        noyaux
                            Orange peel

Stir Lillet, gin and crème de noyaux well with ice.
Strain into prechilled cocktail glass. Twist orange peel
above drink and drop into glass. The scintillating flavor
of Lillet is even more pleasant when this drink is poured
on the rocks.

## NEGRONI

¾ oz. Campari              ¾ oz. sweet vermouth
¾ oz. gin

Stir well with ice. Strain into prechilled cocktail glass.
Similar to the cardinal II except that the vermouth is
sweet instead of dry. May be served on the rocks with
a twist of lemon or splash of soda or both.

## PICON ON THE ROCKS

1½ ozs. Amer Picon          Club soda
½ oz. lemon juice      1  slice lemon

Pour Amer Picon and lemon juice over rocks in prechilled old-fashioned glass. Add a splash of soda. Stir.
Garnish with lemon slice.

# PICON PUNCH

1½ ozs. Amer Picon  |  1  tablespoon cognac
¼ teaspoon grenadine  |  Lemon peel
Iced club soda

Pour Amer Picon, grenadine and a splash of soda over rocks in a prechilled old-fashioned glass. Stir. Float cognac on top of drink. Twist lemon peel above drink and drop into glass. Although Amer Picon is a sweet liqueur, Frenchmen for over a century have sipped it avidly before mealtime. There's just enough bitterness to balance the sweet.

# PLUM APERITIF

1½ ozs. dry vermouth  |  ¼ oz. prunelle
½ oz. cognac  |  1  slice lemon

Stir vermouth, cognac and prunelle well with ice. Strain over rocks in prechilled old-fashioned glass. Add lemon slice. A small jar of fresh beluga caviar will make the *mise en scène* perfect.

# PUNT E MES NEGRONI

¾ oz. Punt e Mes  |  ¾ oz. sweet vermouth
¾ oz. gin

Stir well with ice. Strain into prechilled cocktail glass. May be served on the rocks with a twist of lemon or splash of soda or both. Punt e Mes is one of those Italian aperitifs that cause you first to shudder, then instantly to ask for more.

## RUM APERITIF

| | |
|---|---|
| 1 oz. dry vermouth | 1 teaspoon raspberry |
| 1 oz. light rum | syrup |
| 1 teaspoon dark | ½ oz. lemon juice |
| Jamaican rum | Lemon peel |

Shake vermouth, both kinds of rum, raspberry syrup and lemon juice well with ice. Strain into prechilled cocktail glass. Twist lemon peel above drink and drop into glass. This aperitif could just as well be included among the rum cocktails.

## SANCTUARY

| | |
|---|---|
| 1 oz. Dubonnet | ½ oz. lemon juice |
| ½ oz. Amer Picon | 1 slice lemon |
| ½ oz. Cointreau | |

Shake Dubonnet, Amer Picon, Cointreau and lemon juice well with ice. Strain over rocks in prechilled old-fashioned glass. Add lemon slice. Pass hot hors d'oeuvres.

## SILVER KIRSCH

| | |
|---|---|
| 1½ ozs. Positano | ½ egg white |
| 1 oz. kirsch | 1 teaspoon sugar |
| ½ oz. lemon juice | ⅓ cup crushed ice |

Mix all ingredients in blender for 10 seconds at high speed. Pour into prechilled old-fashioned glass.

## SLOE VERMOUTH

| | |
|---|---|
| 1 oz. sloe gin | 1 oz. dry vermouth |
| (creamy cap) | ½ oz. lemon juice |

Shake well with ice. Strain into prechilled cocktail glass. A soft *divertissement* on a lazy afternoon.

## SOUTHWEST ONE

¾ oz. vodka    ¾ oz. Campari bitters
¾ oz. orange juice

Shake well with ice. Strain into prechilled glass. Named after the London district in which the popular drink originated.

## TRIO

¾ oz. dry vermouth   ¾ oz. gin
¾ oz. sweet vermouth

Stir well with ice. Strain into prechilled cocktail glass.

## VERMOUTH CASSIS

2 ozs. dry vermouth   Iced club soda
1 oz. crème de cassis

Pour vermouth and crème de cassis over one or two rocks in a prechilled old-fashioned glass, a large wine-glass or an 8-oz. highball glass. Stir. Add soda, which Frenchmen use to stretch the drink into a long aperitif. Americans seem to prefer the drink less diluted. A *vin blanc* cassis is the same drink made with dry white wine instead of vermouth. A slice of lemon may be used as a garnish if desired.

## VERMOUTH MARASCHINO

2 ozs. dry vermouth   2 dashes orange
½ oz. maraschino     bitters
 liqueur        1 maraschino cherry
½ oz. lemon juice

Shake vermouth, maraschino liqueur, lemon juice and bitters well with ice. Strain over large ice cube in prechilled old-fashioned glass. Garnish with cherry.

## VERMOUTH TRIPLE SEC

| | |
|---|---|
| *1  oz. dry vermouth* | *2  dashes orange* |
| *½ oz. triple sec* | *bitters* |
| *1  oz. gin* | *Lemon peel* |

Shake vermouth, triple sec, gin and bitters well with ice. Strain into prechilled cocktail glass. Twist lemon peel above drink and drop into glass.

## ZAZA

| | |
|---|---|
| *2  ozs. Dubonnet* | *1  slice orange* |
| *1  oz. gin* | |

Stir Dubonnet and gin well with ice. Strain over rocks in prechilled old-fashioned glass. Cut orange slice in half and place on the rocks. Your nose should catch the aroma of the orange before your lips meet the drink. While there are many versions of this Dubonnet cocktail, these are the proportions we like best.

# Apple-Brandy Cocktails

## APPLE AND GINGER

1¼ ozs. applejack
¾ oz. ginger-flavored
   brandy
½ oz. lemon juice
½ teaspoon sugar

Shake with ice. Strain into prechilled cocktail glass.

## APPLE BLOSSOM

1½ ozs. applejack
1 oz. apple juice
½ oz. lemon juice
1 teaspoon maple
   syrup
⅓ cup crushed ice
1 slice lemon

Put everything except lemon slice into blender. Blend at low speed 10–15 seconds. Pour into prechilled deep-saucer champagne glass. Add lemon slice.

## APPLE DUBONNET

1 oz. calvados
1 oz. Dubonnet
1 slice lemon

Stir calvados and Dubonnet well with ice. Strain over rocks in prechilled old-fashioned glass. Add lemon slice.

## APPLE GRAND MARNIER

1 oz. calvados
½ oz. Grand Marnier
½ oz. cognac
Lemon peel
Orange peel

Stir calvados, Grand Marnier and cognac well with ice. Strain over rocks in prechilled old-fashioned glass. Twist fruit peels above drink and drop into glass.

## APPLE LILLET

1  oz. calvados  1  slice orange
1  oz. Lillet

Stir calvados and Lillet well with ice. Strain over rocks in prechilled old-fashioned glass. Add orange slice. A perfect drink to kill time while waiting for the hot onion soup.

## APPLECAR

¾ oz. applejack  ¾ oz. lemon juice
¾ oz. Cointreau or
  curaçao

Shake well with ice. Strain into prechilled cocktail glass. The appleman's sidecar.

## APPLEHAWK

1¼ ozs. applejack  ½ teaspoon sugar
1¼ ozs. unsweetened
  grapefruit juice

Shake well with ice. Strain into prechilled cocktail glass.

## APPLEJACK MANHATTAN

1¾ ozs. applejack  1  dash orange bitters
¾ oz. sweet vermouth  1  maraschino cherry

Stir applejack, vermouth and bitters well with ice. Strain into prechilled cocktail glass. Add cherry.

## APPLEJACK RABBIT

1½ ozs. applejack
½ oz. lemon juice
½ oz. orange juice

½ teaspoon maple
　syrup

Shake well with ice. Strain into prechilled sugar-frosted cocktail glass. Salted nuts or toasted coconut chips are good companions.

## APPLEJACK SOUR

2 ozs. applejack
½ oz. lemon juice

1 teaspoon sugar
½ slice lemon

Shake applejack, lemon juice and sugar well with ice. Strain into prechilled whiskey-sour glass. Add lemon slice.

## BITTER APPLE

2 ozs. applejack
2 dashes Angostura
　bitters

Iced club soda
Lemon peel

Pour applejack and bitters into prechilled old-fashioned glass. Add ice slices or cubes to fill glass. Add a splash of soda. Stir well. Twist lemon peel above drink and drop into glass. Aromatic, potent and dry.

## BLENHEIM

1 oz. applejack
½ oz. apricot-flavored
　brandy

¾ oz. lemon juice
1 teaspoon grenadine
1 dash orange bitters

Shake well with ice. Strain into prechilled sugar-frosted cocktail glass.

## FROZEN APPLE

| | |
|---|---|
| 1½ ozs. applejack | 1 teaspoon sugar |
| ½ oz. lime juice | ⅓ cup crushed ice |
| ½ egg white | |

Put all ingredients into blender. Blend at low speed 10–15 seconds. Pour into prechilled deep-saucer champagne glass.

## FROZEN APPLE AND BANANA

| | |
|---|---|
| 1½ ozs. applejack | ⅓ cup crushed ice |
| ½ oz. banana liqueur | 1 slice banana |
| ½ oz. lime juice | |

Put applejack, banana liqueur, lime juice and ice into blender. Blend at low speed 10–15 seconds. Pour into prechilled deep-saucer champagne glass. Add banana slice.

## JACK ROSE

| | |
|---|---|
| 2 ozs. applejack | ½ oz. lime juice or |
| 1 teaspoon grenadine | lemon juice |

Shake well with ice. Strain into prechilled cocktail glass. The classic apple-juice drink.

## POLYNESIAN APPLE

| | |
|---|---|
| 1¼ ozs. applejack | ½ oz. California |
| ¾ oz. pineapple juice | brandy |
| | 1 pineapple stick |

Shake applejack, pineapple juice and brandy well with ice. Strain over rocks in prechilled old-fashioned glass. Add pineapple stick. A standby cocktail when spareribs are slowly turning on the spit over charcoal.

## PUERTO APPLE

1¼ ozs. applejack       1½ teaspoons orgeat
 ¾ oz. light rum             or orzata
 ½ oz. lime juice        1  slice lime

Shake applejack, rum, lime juice and orgeat well with ice. Strain over rocks in prechilled old-fashioned glass. Add lime slice.

## RABBIT'S FOOT

¾ oz. apple brandy      ½ oz. lemon juice
¾ oz. light rum          ¼ oz. grenadine
½ oz. orange juice       1  slice orange

Mix apple brandy, rum, orange juice, lemon juice and grenadine well with ice. Strain into prechilled old-fashioned glass. Add ice to fill glass. Garnish with orange slice. Created by Roy Devlin, head bartender at the Cincinnati Playboy Club.

# Brandy Cocktails

## ALABAMA

1¾ ozs. brandy
½ oz. lemon juice
1 teaspoon curaçao

½ teaspoon sugar
Orange peel

Shake brandy, lemon juice, curaçao and sugar well with ice. Strain into prechilled sugar-frosted cocktail glass. Twist orange peel above drink and drop into glass.

## BAYOU

1¾ ozs. brandy
¼ oz. peach liqueur
½ oz. mango nectar

2 teaspoons lime juice
1 slice fresh or
    brandied peach

Shake brandy, peach liqueur, mango nectar and lime juice well with ice. Strain over rocks in prechilled old-fashioned glass. Garnish with peach slice.

## BOMBAY

1 oz. brandy
½ oz. dry vermouth
½ oz. sweet vermouth
½ teaspoon curaçao

¼ teaspoon Pernod
1 slice fresh or
    canned mango

Shake brandy, both kinds of vermouth, curaçao and Pernod well with ice. Strain over rocks in prechilled old-fashioned glass. Add mango slice. Serve before a curry dinner.

# BRANDIED APRICOT

1½ ozs. brandy          ½ oz. lemon juice
½ oz. apricot-flavored  Orange peel
    brandy

Shake brandy, apricot-flavored brandy and lemon juice
with ice. Strain into prechilled sugar-frosted cocktail
glass. Twist orange peel above drink and drop into glass.

# BRANDIED CORDIAL MEDOC

1½ ozs. brandy          ½ oz. lemon juice
½ oz. Cordial Médoc     Orange peel

Shake brandy, Cordial Médoc and lemon juice well with
ice. Strain into prechilled cocktail glass. Twist orange
peel above drink and drop into glass.

# BRANDIED GINGER

2 ozs. brandy           1 teaspoon orange
½ oz. ginger-flavored       juice
    brandy              1 piece preserved
1 teaspoon lime juice       ginger in syrup

Shake brandy, ginger-flavored brandy, lime juice and
orange juice well with ice. Strain over rocks in prechilled old-fashioned glass. Garnish with ginger.

# BRANDTINI

1½ ozs. brandy          Lemon peel or
1 oz. gin                   cocktail olive
1 teaspoon dry
    vermouth

Stir brandy, gin and vermouth well with ice. Strain into
prechilled cocktail glass. Twist lemon peel above drink
and drop into glass, or serve with cocktail olive.

## BRANDY ALEXANDER

¾ oz. brandy               ¾ oz. cream
¾ oz. crème de cacao

Shake well with ice. Strain into prechilled cocktail glass.

## BRANDY AND AMER PICON

2  ozs. cognac            Lemon peel
½ oz. Amer Picon          Orange peel

Stir cognac and Amer Picon well with ice. Strain over rocks in prechilled old-fashioned glass. Twist lemon peel and orange peel above drink and drop into glass.

## BRANDY CASSIS

1¾ ozs. brandy           2  teaspoons crème de
¾ oz. lemon juice           cassis
                          Lemon peel

Shake brandy, lemon juice and crème de cassis well with ice. Strain into prechilled cocktail glass. Twist lemon peel above drink and drop into glass.

## BRANDY CRUSTA

Peel of ½ lemon, in    2  teaspoons lemon
   one spiral              juice
2  ozs. brandy         1  dash bitters
½ oz. curaçao          1  teaspoon maraschino
                          liqueur

Place lemon peel and cracked ice or rocks in prechilled sugar-frosted old-fashioned glass. Shake brandy, curaçao, lemon juice, bitters and maraschino liqueur well with ice. Strain into glass.

# BRANDY FINO

1½ ozs. brandy          ½ slice orange
½ oz. very dry sherry      Lemon peel
½ oz. Drambuie

Shake brandy, sherry and Drambuie well with ice. Strain over rocks in prechilled old-fashioned glass. Add orange slice. Twist lemon peel above drink and drop into glass.

# BRANDY GUMP

2 ozs. brandy          ½ teaspoon grenadine
½ oz. lemon juice

Shake well with ice. Strain into prechilled cocktail glass. A good one to relax with after an all-day sail.

# BRANDY MANHATTAN

2 ozs. brandy          1 dash bitters
½ oz. sweet vermouth        (optional)
                  1 maraschino cherry

Stir brandy, vermouth and bitters well with ice. Strain into prechilled cocktail glass. Add cherry. For a dry brandy manhattan, use dry instead of sweet vermouth.

# BRANDY MELBA

1½ ozs. brandy          ½ oz. lemon juice
¼ oz. peach liqueur      2 dashes orange bitters
¼ oz. raspberry        1 slice brandied peach
    liqueur

Shake brandy, peach liqueur, raspberry liqueur, lemon juice and bitters well with ice. Strain into prechilled cocktail glass. Add peach slice. If raspberry liqueur isn't available, raspberry syrup may be substituted.

# BRANDY SOUR

2  ozs. brandy
½ oz. lemon juice
¼ oz. orange juice

½ to 1 teaspoon sugar
½ slice lemon

Shake brandy, lemon juice, orange juice and sugar well with ice. Strain into prechilled whiskey-sour glass. Add lemon slice. Softer than a whiskey sour.

# CHAMPS ELYSEES

1½ ozs. cognac
½ oz. Chartreuse
½ oz. lemon juice

1  dash Angostura
    bitters (optional)

Shake well with ice. Strain over rocks in prechilled old-fashioned glass. Bitters may be omitted for a more pronounced Chartreuse flavor.

# CHERRY BLOSSOM

1¼ ozs. brandy
¾ oz. wild-cherry
    liqueur

¼ teaspoon curaçao
¼ teaspoon grenadine
2  teaspoons lemon
    juice

Shake well with ice. Strain into prechilled sugar-frosted cocktail glass. Rub rim of glass with wild-cherry liqueur before dipping into sugar.

# CLASSIC

1½ ozs. brandy
½ oz. lemon juice

¼ oz. maraschino
    liqueur
¼ oz. curaçao

Shake well with ice. Strain into prechilled cocktail glass. More tart than earlier versions of the brandy classic.

## DEAUVILLE

*1  oz. brandy*            *½ oz. apple brandy*
*½ oz. lemon juice*        *½ oz. triple sec*

Shake with ice. Strain into prechilled cocktail glass.


## DRY COLD DECK

*1¾ ozs. brandy*           *¼ oz. white crème de*
*½ oz. dry vermouth*            *menthe*

Shake well with ice. Strain into prechilled cocktail glass.
A sophisticated stinger.


## FEMINA

*1½ ozs. brandy*           *1  slice cocktail orange*
*½ oz. Benedictine*            *in syrup*
*½ oz. orange juice*

Shake brandy, Benedictine and orange juice well with
ice. Strain over rocks in prechilled old-fashioned glass.
Add orange slice.


## FOXHOUND

*1½ ozs. brandy*           *1  teaspoon lemon*
*½ oz. cranberry juice*        *juice*
*1  teaspoon kümmel*       *½ slice lemon*

Shake brandy, cranberry juice, kümmel and lemon juice
well with ice. Strain over rocks in prechilled old-
fashioned glass. Add lemon slice.

## FROUPE

| | |
|---|---|
| 1¼ ozs. brandy | 1 teaspoon |
| 1¼ ozs. sweet | Benedictine |
| vermouth | |

Stir well with ice. Strain into prechilled cocktail glass.
Like a sunset's afterglow.

## FROZEN BRANDY AND PORT

| | |
|---|---|
| 1½ ozs. brandy | 1 teaspoon powdered |
| 1 oz. port | sugar |
| 1 small egg | ⅓ cup crushed ice |
| | Grated nutmeg |

Put brandy, port, egg, sugar and ice into blender. Blend
20 seconds at low speed. Pour into prechilled saucer
champagne glass. Sprinkle with nutmeg. Also known as
coffee flip when crushed ice is omitted and drink is
shaken with ice in regular cocktail shaker.

## FROZEN BRANDY AND RUM

| | |
|---|---|
| 1½ ozs. brandy | 1 egg yolk |
| 1 oz. golden rum | 1½ teaspoons sugar |
| ½ oz. lemon juice | ⅓ cup crushed ice |

Put all ingredients into blender. Blend 15–20 seconds
at low speed. Pour into prechilled saucer champagne
glass. Soothing.

## HARVARD

| | |
|---|---|
| 1½ ozs. brandy | 1 teaspoon grenadine |
| ½ oz. dry vermouth | 2 teaspoons lemon juice |

Shake well with ice. Strain into prechilled cocktail glass.
Drier than earlier versions, but still crimson.

## JAPANESE

2  ozs. brandy
¼ oz. orgeat or orzata
¼ oz. lime juice

1  dash Angostura
    bitters
Lime peel

Shake brandy, orgeat, lime juice and bitters well with ice. Strain into prechilled cocktail glass. Twist lime peel above drink and drop into glass.

## LA JOLLA

1½ ozs. brandy
½ oz. banana liqueur
2  teaspoons lemon
    juice

1  teaspoon orange
    juice

Shake well with ice. Strain into prechilled sugar-frosted cocktail glass.

## McBRANDY

1½ ozs. brandy
1  oz. apple juice

1  teaspoon lemon
    juice
1  slice lemon

Shake brandy, apple juice and lemon juice well with ice. Strain into prechilled cocktail glass. Add lemon slice. Serve before a dinner of roast ham or duck.

## PHOEBE SNOW

1¼ ozs. brandy
1¼ ozs. Dubonnet

¼ teaspoon Pernod

Shake well with ice. Strain into prechilled cocktail glass.

## PICASSO

| | |
|---|---|
| *1½ ozs. cognac* | *1 teaspoon sugar* |
| *½ oz. Dubonnet* | *Orange peel* |
| *½ oz. lime juice* | |

Shake cognac, Dubonnet, lime juice and sugar well with ice. Strain into prechilled cocktail glass. Twist orange peel above drink and drop into glass.

## POLONAISE

| | |
|---|---|
| *1½ ozs. brandy* | *½ oz. very dry sherry* |
| *½ oz. blackberry liqueur or black- berry-flavored brandy* | *1 teaspoon lemon juice* |
| | *2 dashes orange bitters* |

Shake well with ice. Strain over rocks in prechilled old-fashioned glass.

## QUAKER

| | |
|---|---|
| *1½ ozs. brandy* | *1 teaspoon raspberry syrup or grenadine* |
| *½ oz. rum* | |
| *½ oz. lemon juice* | *Lemon peel* |

Shake liquids with ice. Strain into prechilled cocktail glass. Twist lemon peel above drink and drop into glass. Two rounds of these and all will be Friends.

## SANTA FE

| | |
|---|---|
| *1½ ozs. brandy* | *1 teaspoon lemon juice* |
| *½ oz. grapefruit juice* | |
| *½ oz. dry vermouth* | |

Shake all ingredients well with ice. Strain into pre-chilled sugar-rimmed cocktail glass.

COCKTAILS 51

## SARATOGA

2 ozs. brandy
½ oz. pineapple juice
1 teaspoon lemon
    juice

½ teaspoon
    maraschino
    liqueur
1 dash Angostura
    bitters

Shake with ice. Strain into prechilled cocktail glass.

## SIDECAR

¾ oz. brandy
¾ oz. curaçao

¾ oz. lemon juice

Shake well with ice. Strain into prechilled cocktail glass.
All three ingredients may be varied to suit one's taste.
One of the most venerable of classic cocktails.

## SLOE BRANDY

2 ozs. brandy
½ oz. sloe gin
    (creamy cap)

1 teaspoon lemon
    juice
Lemon peel

Shake brandy, sloe gin and lemon juice well with ice.
Strain into prechilled cocktail glass. Twist lemon peel
above drink and drop into glass.

## SOUTH PACIFIC

1½ ozs. brandy
½ oz. lemon juice
¼ oz. crème d'ananas

¼ oz. white crème de
    menthe
1 pineapple stick

Shake brandy, lemon juice, crème d'ananas and crème
de menthe well with ice. Strain over rocks in prechilled
old-fashioned glass. Garnish with pineapple stick. In
place of the two liqueurs, you may use Hawaiian
minted-pineapple liqueur.

## STINGER

1¼ ozs. brandy          1¼ ozs. white crème
                                      de menthe

Shake well with ice. Strain into prechilled cocktail glass.
For a dry stinger, increase brandy to 2 ozs. and reduce
crème de menthe to ½ oz. May be offered before or
after dinner. It is frequently served with a glass of ice
water on the side.

## THUMPER

1¾ ozs. brandy          Lemon peel
 ¾ oz. Tuaca liqueur

Stir brandy and Tuaca well with ice. Strain into prechilled old-fashioned glass. Add ice cubes or ice slices to
fill glass. Stir well. Twist lemon peel above drink and
drop into glass. One of Italy's oldest liqueurs shines in
this drink.

## VIA VENETO

1¾ ozs. brandy          2  teaspoons lemon
 ½ oz. sambuca              juice
 ½ egg white            1  teaspoon sugar

Shake well with ice. Strain over rocks in prechilled old-
fashioned glass. An engaging patio drink that's a little
on the sweet side.

## WATERBURY

1½ ozs. brandy          ½ teaspoon grenadine
 ½ oz. lime juice       ½ teaspoon powdered
 ½ egg white               sugar

Shake well with ice. Strain into prechilled sugar-frosted
cocktail glass.

# Champagne Cocktails

## AMERICANA

| | |
|---|---|
| 1   teaspoon 100-proof bourbon | 4   ozs. iced brut champagne |
| ½ teaspoon sugar | 1   slice fresh or brandied peach |
| 1   dash bitters | |

Stir bourbon, sugar and bitters in prechilled champagne glass. Add champagne and peach slice.

## CARIBBEAN CHAMPAGNE

| | |
|---|---|
| ½ teaspoon light rum | 4   ozs. iced brut champagne |
| ½ teaspoon banana liqueur | 1   slice banana |
| 1   dash orange bitters | |

Pour rum, banana liqueur and bitters into prechilled champagne glass. Add champagne. Stir very gently. Add banana slice.

## CHAMPAGNE FRAISE

| | |
|---|---|
| ½ teaspoon strawberry liqueur | 4   ozs. iced brut champagne |
| ½ teaspoon kirsch | 1   large fresh strawberry |

Pour strawberry liqueur and kirsch into prechilled champagne glass. Tilt glass so that liqueurs coat bottom and sides of glass. Add champagne. Float strawberry on drink. (Measure ½ teaspoons precisely—don't over-pour.)

## CHAMPAGNE MANHATTAN

1    oz. Canadian whisky      3    ozs. iced brut
¼    oz. sweet vermouth            champagne
1    dash bitters             1    brandied cherry

Stir whisky, vermouth and bitters well with ice. Strain
into prechilled champagne glass. Add champagne and
brandied cherry.

## CHAMPAGNE NORMANDE

1    teaspoon calvados        4    ozs. iced brut
½    teaspoon sugar                champagne
1    dash Angostura
     bitters

Stir calvados, sugar and bitters in prechilled champagne
glass. Add champagne. Stir very gently.

## CHAMPAGNE NOYAUX

½    oz. crème de             4    ozs. iced brut
     noyaux                        champagne
1    teaspoon lime juice      1    slice lime
1    large toasted almond

Stir crème de noyaux and lime juice in prechilled champagne glass. Add almond. Pour champagne into glass.
Stir slightly. Float lime slice on top.

## CHAMPAGNE OLD-FASHIONED

½    oz. Grand Marnier        4    ozs. iced brut
½    oz. Forbidden Fruit           champagne
1    dash orange bitters      1    slice lemon

Into prechilled old-fashioned glass, pour liqueurs and
bitters. Fill glass with champagne. Stir very gently.
Launch with lemon slice.

# CHAMPAGNE POLONAISE

| | |
|---|---|
| *1  teaspoon blackberry liqueur (Polish is best)* | *½  teaspoon cognac*<br>*4  ozs. iced brut champagne* |

Pour blackberry liqueur and cognac into prechilled sugar-frosted champagne glass. Add champagne. Stir very gently.

# CHARTREUSE CHAMPAGNE

| | |
|---|---|
| *½  teaspoon green Chartreuse*<br>*½  teaspoon cognac* | *4  ozs. iced brut champagne*<br>*Lemon peel* |

Pour Chartreuse, cognac and champagne into prechilled champagne glass. Stir very gently. Twist lemon peel above drink and drop into glass. Toast the Carthusians.

# CHERRY CHAMPAGNE

| | |
|---|---|
| *½  oz. iced Cherry Heering* | *4  ozs. iced brut champagne*<br>*½  pitted fresh cherry* |

Pour Cherry Heering into hollow of prechilled hollow-stemmed champagne glass. Add champagne. Float cherry on drink.

# CLASSIC CHAMPAGNE COCKTAIL

| | |
|---|---|
| *½  teaspoon sugar*<br>*1  dash Angostura bitters* | *4  ozs. iced brut champagne*<br>*Lemon peel* |

Stir sugar and bitters in prechilled champagne glass. Add champagne. Usually, the sparkle of the champagne will blend the ingredients, and little stirring is necessary. Twist lemon peel above drink and drop into glass.

## MELBA CHAMPAGNE

½ oz. Himbeergeist (raspberry brandy, not liqueur)

4 ozs. iced brut champagne

1 fresh or thawed frozen raspberry Raspberry sherbet, hard-frozen

Pour Himbeergeist into prechilled champagne glass. Add champagne and the raspberry. With a fruit-baller, scoop out a single small ball of sherbet. Float on champagne.

## ORANGE CHAMPAGNE

Peel of ½ orange, in one spiral

2 teaspoons curaçao

4 ozs. iced brut champagne

Place orange peel in prechilled champagne glass. Add curaçao and champagne. Stir very gently.

## SPARKLING GALLIANO

½ oz. Galliano
½ teaspoon lemon juice
4 ozs. iced brut champagne

Cucumber peel, 1½ inches long, ½ inch wide

Pour Galliano and lemon juice into prechilled champagne glass. Stir. Add champagne and cucumber peel. Drink to the stars.

# Gin Cocktails

### ALEXANDER WITH COFFEE

¾ oz. gin            ¾ oz. cream
¾ oz. coffee liqueur

Shake well with ice. Strain into prechilled sugar-frosted cocktail glass. Moisten rim of glass with coffee liqueur before dipping into sugar. Especially good with espresso-coffee liqueur or Galacafe.

### ALEXANDER WITH GIN

¾ oz. gin            ¾ oz. cream
¾ oz. crème de cacao

Shake well with ice. Strain into prechilled cocktail glass. (Alexanders made with a brandy base instead of gin will be found among brandy cocktails.)

### ALEXANDER WITH PRUNELLE

¾ oz. gin            ¾ oz. cream
¾ oz. prunelle        Ground cinnamon

Shake gin, prunelle and cream well with ice. Strain into prechilled cocktail glass. Sprinkle lightly with cinnamon.

### ALEXANDER'S SISTER

¾ oz. gin            ¾ oz. cream
¾ oz. white or green
    crème de menthe

Shake well with ice. Strain into prechilled cocktail glass.

## BENNETT

1½ ozs. gin
½ oz. lime juice
½ teaspoon sugar

2 dashes Angostura
   bitters
Lime peel

Shake gin, lime juice, sugar and bitters well with ice. Strain into prechilled cocktail glass. Twist lime peel above drink and drop into glass.

## BERLINER

1½ ozs. gin
¼ oz. dry kümmel

½ oz. dry vermouth
¼ oz. lemon juice

Shake well with ice. Strain into prechilled cocktail glass. Best appreciated with freshly made, well-buttered smoked-salmon canapés.

## BISCAYNE

1 oz. gin
½ oz. light rum
½ oz. Forbidden Fruit

½ oz. lime juice
1 slice lime

Shake gin, rum, Forbidden Fruit and lime juice well with ice. Strain over rocks in prechilled old-fashioned glass. Add lime slice.

## BLUE DEVIL

1½ ozs. gin
½ oz. blue curaçao

½ oz. lemon juice
1 slice lemon

Shake gin, curaçao and lemon juice well with ice. Strain into prechilled cocktail glass garnished with lemon slice. A gentle blues chaser.

## BONNIE PRINCE

1¼ ozs. gin        ¼ oz. Drambuie
½ oz. Lillet

Shake well with ice. Strain into prechilled cocktail glass. Inspired by gin drinkers with both French and Scottish blood in their veins.

## BRITTANY

1½ ozs. gin        ¼ oz. lemon juice
½ oz. Amer Picon        Orange peel
¼ oz. orange juice

Shake gin, Amer Picon, orange juice and lemon juice well with ice. Strain into prechilled cocktail glass. Twist orange peel above drink and drop into glass.

## BRONX

1½ ozs. gin        ¼ oz. dry vermouth
½ oz. orange juice        ¼ oz. sweet vermouth

Shake well with ice. Strain into prechilled cocktail glass. For a drier bronx, omit sweet vermouth and increase gin to 1¾ ozs. One of the few inventions of the Prohibition era really worth retaining when made with fine gin rather than the notorious bathtub variety.

## CHATHAM

1¼ ozs. gin        1 small piece
½ oz. ginger-flavored        preserved ginger
    brandy             in syrup
¼ oz. lemon juice

Shake gin, ginger-flavored brandy and lemon juice well with ice. Strain into prechilled cocktail glass. Garnish with preserved ginger.

## CHERRY SLING

1½ ozs. gin                ½ oz. lime juice
½ oz. cherry liqueur

Shake well with ice. Strain into prechilled cocktail glass.
Use a tart cherry liqueur such as Cherry Heering or
the domestic Cherry Karise for best results.

## CLOISTER

1½ ozs. gin                ¼ oz. yellow
½ oz. grapefruit juice        Chartreuse
¼ oz. lemon juice

Shake well with ice. Strain into prechilled cocktail glass.
A contemplative kind of drink, perfect for an autumn
sundown.

## CLOVER CLUB

1½ ozs. gin                1  teaspoon grenadine
¾ oz. lemon juice               or raspberry
                                syrup
                            ½ egg white

Shake well with ice. Strain into prechilled cocktail glass.

## CLOVER CLUB ROYAL

1½ ozs. gin                1  teaspoon grenadine
¾ oz. lemon juice               or raspberry syrup
                            ½ egg yolk

Shake well with ice. Strain into prechilled cocktail glass.
A trifle richer than the clover club, above, this velvety
cocktail is even smoother when made with ⅓ cup
crushed ice in a blender and poured over the rocks in
an old-fashioned glass.

## COCONUT GIN

1½ ozs. gin
½ oz. lemon juice
¼ oz. maraschino
    syrup

¼ oz. cream of
    coconut

Cream of coconut, from the can, should be well mixed before using. Shake all ingredients well with ice. Strain into prechilled sugar-frosted cocktail glass. Sets up a beautiful indoor tropical breeze.

## COLD GIN TODDY

2 ozs. gin
½ teaspoon sugar

Lemon peel

Shake gin and sugar well with plenty of ice and strain into old-fashioned glass filled with large cubes or slices of ice. Twist lemon peel above drink and drop into glass.

## COPENHAGEN

1 oz. gin
1 oz. aquavit

¼ oz. dry vermouth
1 large stuffed olive

Stir gin, aquavit and vermouth well with ice. Strain into prechilled cocktail glass. Add olive.

## CORDIAL MEDOC

1 oz. gin
½ oz. Cordial Médoc

½ oz. dry vermouth
¼ oz. lemon juice

Shake well with ice. Strain into prechilled cocktail glass. For a bon-voyage cocktail party before flying to Paris.

## CORDIAL MEDOC SOUR

1½ ozs. gin      ½ oz. lemon juice
½ oz. Cordial Médoc      ½ slice orange

Shake gin, Cordial Médoc and lemon juice well with ice. Strain into prechilled whiskey-sour glass. Garnish with orange slice.

## DUNDEE

1   oz. gin      ¼ oz. lemon juice
½ oz. Scotch      Lemon peel
½ oz. Drambuie

Shake gin, Scotch, Drambuie and lemon juice well with ice. Pour over rocks in prechilled old-fashioned glass. Twist lemon peel above drink and drop into glass.

## FOGGY DAY

1½ ozs. gin      1   slice lemon
¼ oz. Pernod      Lemon peel

Shake gin and Pernod well with ice. Strain into prechilled old-fashioned glass. Add ice to fill glass. Rub outside of lemon peel around rim of glass and drop peel into glass. Add lemon slice. Created by Jerry Wyman, head bartender at the Phoenix Playboy Club.

## GENOA

¾ oz. gin      ½ oz. dry vermouth
¾ oz. grappa      1   olive
½ oz. sambuca

Stir gin, grappa, sambuca and vermouth well with ice. Strain into prechilled cocktail glass. Add olive.

## GIMLET

2 ozs. gin
   or vodka

½ oz. Rose's lime
   juice

Stir extremely well with ice. Strain into prechilled cocktail glass. Long stirring is absolutely essential to present this English classic in its best light. Glass may be sugar-frosted by moistening rim with Rose's lime juice before dipping into sugar.

## GIN AND LIME

1½ ozs. gin
½ oz. fresh lime juice
½ oz. orange juice

1 teaspoon Rose's
   lime juice
Lime peel

Shake gin, fresh lime juice, orange juice and Rose's lime juice well with ice. Strain into prechilled cocktail glass. Twist lime peel above drink and drop into glass.

## GIN AQUAVIT

1½ ozs. gin
½ oz. aquavit
½ oz. lemon juice
1 teaspoon sugar

½ egg white
1 teaspoon heavy
   cream

Shake well with ice. Strain into prechilled old-fashioned glass containing two or three ice cubes. A light, foamy drink to serve before passing a platter of Danish open sandwiches.

## GIN CASSIS

1½ ozs. gin
½ oz. lemon juice

½ oz. crème de cassis

Shake well with ice. Strain into prechilled cocktail glass, or into old-fashioned glass with one or two rocks.

# GIN DAIQUIRI

1½ ozs. gin                ½ oz. lime juice
½ oz. light rum            ½ teaspoon sugar

Shake well with ice. Strain into prechilled sugar-frosted cocktail glass.

# GIN OLD-FASHIONED

¼ teaspoon sugar           1¾ ozs. gin
1 or 2 dashes              Lemon peel
  Angostura bitters

Put sugar and bitters into prechilled old-fashioned glass. Stir until sugar dissolves, adding a teaspoon of water if necessary to complete the process. Add gin and two or three ice cubes or large pieces of coarsely cracked ice. Stir well. Twist lemon peel above drink and drop into glass. Old-fashioneds are frequently garnished with orange slice, lemon slice, pineapple, cherry, etc., but knowledgeable old-fashioned men shun the fruit salad.

# GIN SIDECAR

¾ oz. high-proof           ¾ oz. triple sec
  English gin              ¾ oz. lemon juice

Shake well with ice. Strain into prechilled cocktail glass.

# GIN SOUR

1½ ozs. gin                1 teaspoon sugar
½ oz. lemon juice          ½ slice orange
¼ oz. orange juice         1 maraschino cherry

Shake gin, lemon juice, orange juice and sugar well with ice. Strain into prechilled whiskey-sour glass. Garnish with orange slice and cherry.

## GIN SOUTHERN

1½ ozs. gin
½ oz. Southern
   Comfort
¼ oz. grapefruit
   juice
¼ oz. lemon juice

Shake well with ice. Strain into prechilled cocktail glass. For drinking men who appreciate verandas and magnolia blossoms.

## GOLDEN HORNET

1½ ozs. gin
½ oz. amontillado
   sherry
½ oz. Scotch
Lemon peel

Stir gin and sherry well with ice. Strain over two rocks in prechilled old-fashioned glass. Float Scotch on top. Twist lemon peel over drink and drop into glass. Created by Tom Moore, head bartender at the New York Playboy Club.

## GRANVILLE

1½ ozs. gin
¼ oz. Grand Marnier
¼ oz. calvados
¼ oz. lemon juice

Shake with ice. Strain into prechilled cocktail glass.

## GREEN DEVIL

1½ ozs. gin
½ oz. lime juice
¼ oz. green crème
   de menthe
2 sprigs mint

Shake gin, lime juice and crème de menthe well with ice. Strain over two or three rocks in prechilled old-fashioned glass. Tear several mint leaves to release aroma before adding to drink as garnish.

## HUDSON BAY

| | |
|---|---|
| 1   oz. gin | ¼ oz. lime juice |
| ½ oz. cherry liqueur | ¼ oz. 151-proof rum |
| ½ oz. orange juice | 1   slice lime |

Shake gin, cherry liqueur, orange juice, lime juice and rum well with ice. Strain into prechilled cocktail glass. Add lime slice. A winter or summer cocktail.

## JAMAICA GLOW

| | |
|---|---|
| 1½ ozs. gin | 1   teaspoon dark |
| ½ oz. dry red wine |       Jamaican rum |
| ½ oz. orange juice | 1   slice lime |

Shake gin, wine, orange juice and rum well with ice. Strain into prechilled sugar-frosted cocktail glass. Add lime slice. This relic of plantation days is still a magnificent reviver for surf riders and scuba divers.

## JOULOUVILLE

| | |
|---|---|
| 1   oz. gin | ¼ oz. sweet |
| ½ oz. apple brandy |       vermouth |
| ½ oz. lemon juice | ¼ teaspoon grenadine |

Shake well with ice. Strain into prechilled cocktail glass.

## KEY COCKTAIL

| | |
|---|---|
| 1½ ozs. gin | ¼ oz. dark Jamaican |
| ½ oz. lime juice |       rum |
| ¼ oz. Falernum | 1   pineapple stick |

Shake gin, lime juice, Falernum and rum well with ice. Strain into prechilled cocktail glass. Garnish with pineapple stick.

# MARTINI

Over the years, the martini, most famous of all cock-tail-hour thoroughbreds, has evolved into a drink that is practically all gin with only the faintest hint of vermouth. This preference for drier and drier martinis (while *dry* usually means less sweet, in reference to martinis it means less vermouth) has spawned some strange equipment and a countless number of jokes. Some barmen ritualize the exacting vermouth formula with a long Rx dropper; some spray their vermouth from atomizers. The fanatical, reaching the *reductio ad absurdum,* claim they waft the vermouth bottletop over the gin or mutter the word *vermouth* under their breath while stirring their raw concoction in the mixing glass. It would be unfortunate if the use of vermouth in the martini became extinct, for its bite, however faint, is trenchant. It turns cold gin into a civilized cocktail.

Most top-flight barmen make their martinis with about ten or twelve parts gin to one part dry vermouth. The drink may be served "up," meaning in a regular stemmed cocktail glass, or on the rocks in an old-fashioned glass. You can drop a twist of lemon peel into the glass or rub the rim with the peel before adding it to the drink. The martini's most common garnish is an olive, pitted or stuffed. With a cocktail-onion garnish, it turns into a gibson.

A martini must be piercingly cold; at its best, both gin and vermouth are prechilled in the refrigerator, well stirred with ice and poured into a prechilled glass. Energetic stirring with the ice is all-important; the dilution makes the drink both smooth and palatable. Those who merely combine gin and vermouth before-hand and then refrigerate without stirring wind up serving raw slugs to guests who are quickly cargoed and who completely miss the pleasure of a well-made martini.

Although vermouth is the spirited minor ingredient, a bottle opened for pouring and left standing in the liquor cabinet for weeks will lose its bell-ringing zest. To retain as much as possible of the flavor of the aromatic herbs used in making vermouth, store the opened bottle in the refrigerator. It's a good idea for the martini man to buy his vermouth in pint bottles and make frequent replacements.

Here are several variations on the familiar martini theme:

## 12-TO-1 MARTINI

| | |
|---|---|
| 2 ozs. gin | 1 teaspoon dry vermouth |

## 8-TO-1 MARTINI

| | |
|---|---|
| 2 ozs. gin | ¼ oz. dry vermouth |

## 4-TO-1 MARTINI

| | |
|---|---|
| 2 ozs. gin | ½ oz. dry vermouth |

## GIBSON

As noted, any of the above martini mixtures garnished with a cocktail onion.

## BLENTON

| | |
|---|---|
| 1½ ozs. gin | 1 dash Angostura bitters |
| ¾ oz. dry vermouth | |

Stir well with ice. Strain into prechilled cocktail glass. A martini variation so old that it's new.

# BLOODHOUND

| | |
|---|---|
| *1 oz. gin* | *½ oz. strawberry* |
| *½ oz. dry vermouth* | *liqueur* |
| *½ oz. sweet vermouth* | *1 large strawberry* |

Shake gin, both kinds of vermouth and strawberry liqueur well with ice. Strain into prechilled cocktail glass. Drop strawberry into glass. The best dry vermouth for this one is Chambery fraise.

# FINO MARTINI

*2 ozs. gin*                    *½ oz. fino sherry*

Stir well with ice. Strain into prechilled cocktail glass. Add olive or lemon twist. Serve with a side dish of freshly toasted, salted almonds.

# FLYING DUTCHMAN

*2 ozs. gin*                         *Curaçao*

Stir gin well with ice. Into a prechilled cocktail glass, pour enough curaçao so that when the glass is slowly twirled, it will coat the sides. Add the gin.

# GIN AND IT

*2 ozs. gin*                    *Italian sweet*
*vermouth*

Stir gin well with ice. Into a prechilled cocktail glass, pour enough vermouth so that when the glass is slowly twirled, it will coat the sides. Add the gin. The English drink is often served at room temperature. The *It* stands for the Italian vermouth. A gin and French is the same drink with French dry vermouth instead.

## KNICKERBOCKER

2   ozs. gin                    ¼ oz. sweet vermouth
½ oz. dry vermouth

Stir well with ice. Strain into prechilled cocktail glass.
Serve without benefit of cherry, olive or lemon twist.
This version of the martini appeals to those who like
vermouth in both sweet and dry forms.

## MARSALA MARTINI

¾ oz. gin                    ¾ oz. dry Marsala
¾ oz. dry vermouth           Lemon peel

Stir gin, vermouth and Marsala well with ice. Strain
into prechilled cocktail glass. Twist lemon peel above
drink and drop into glass.

## MARTINEZ

2   ozs. gin                  ½ oz. dry vermouth
½ teaspoon                   2 dashes orange
    maraschino liqueur          bitters

Stir well with ice. Strain into prechilled cocktail glass.
Martini men with a strain of Spanish in their veins go
for this one. Alleged to have been the original martini.

## MARTINI, HOLLAND STYLE

2   ozs. Dutch genever       ½ oz. dry vermouth
    gin                       Lemon peel

Stir gin and vermouth well with ice. Strain into prechilled cocktail glass. Twist lemon peel above drink
and drop into glass.

## PAISLEY MARTINI

2¼ ozs. gin              1  teaspoon Scotch
 ¼ oz. dry vermouth

Stir well with ice. Strain into prechilled cocktail glass.
The flavor of the Scotch in this 9-to-1 martini is just
subtle enough to let the drinker know that something
delightfully offbeat is in his glass.

## PERFECT

1½ ozs. gin              ½ oz. sweet vermouth
 ½ oz. dry vermouth

Stir well with ice. Strain into prechilled cocktail glass.
Add olive or twist of lemon peel if desired. Modern
martini men would call this an "imperfect" martini,
but *perfect* is its traditional name.

## PERNOD MARTINI

2  ozs. gin              ⅛ teaspoon Pernod
 ½ oz. dry vermouth

Stir well with ice. Strain into prechilled cocktail glass.
Very pleasant with an onion-stuffed olive. Some bartenders pour a soupçon of Pernod into the glass, swirl
it around and then add the martini.

## RACQUET CLUB

2  ozs. gin              2  dashes orange bitters
 ½ oz. dry vermouth

Shake, don't stir, with ice in silver cocktail shaker
until shaker is completely frosted. Strain into cocktail
glass so cold it's somewhat uncomfortable to hold.

# SAKETINI

2 ozs. gin                    ½ oz. sake

Stir well with ice. Strain into prechilled cocktail glass.
If desired, an olive or twist of lemon peel may be
added. The saketini is a reminder that dry vermouth
and rice wine bear an uncanny resemblance to each
other.

# SWEET MARTINI

2 ozs. gin                    Orange peel
½ oz. sweet vermouth

Stir gin and vermouth well with ice. Strain into prechilled cocktail glass. Twist orange peel above drink
and drop into glass. While *sweet martini* sounds like a
contradiction in terms, the drink is not only tolerable
but titillating.

# MATINEE

1 oz. gin                    1 teaspoon heavy
½ oz. sambuca                    cream
½ egg white                    ½ oz. lime juice

Shake all ingredients well with ice. Strain into prechilled
cocktail glass. A comfortable midafternoon cocktail.
May also be served as a pick-me-up the morning after
with a spray of freshly ground nutmeg.

## MINTED GIN

1½ ozs. gin                1  slice lemon
½ oz. lemon juice          ½  slice orange
½ teaspoon sugar           2  sprigs fresh mint

Shake gin, lemon juice and sugar well with ice. Strain into prechilled old-fashioned glass with rocks. Garnish drink with lemon and orange slices. Tear mint leaves before placing on rocks. A perfect drink for unwinding after 18 holes on the fairway.

## MOLDAU

1½ ozs. gin                ¼  oz. lemon juice
½ oz. plum brandy          1  brandied cherry
¼ oz. orange juice

Shake gin, plum brandy, orange juice and lemon juice well with ice. Strain into prechilled old-fashioned glass with two or three ice cubes. Garnish with brandied cherry.

## MORRO

1  oz. gin                 ½  oz. pineapple
½ oz. golden rum              juice
½ oz. lime juice           ½  teaspoon sugar

Shake well with ice. Strain into prechilled sugar-frosted glass. Moisten rim of glass with Falernum before dipping into sugar. Once tasted, the marriage of gin and rum is one of those unions that no man in his right drinking sense would dream of putting asunder. Fruit juices in this drink help fortify the nuptials.

## ORANGE BLOSSOM

1½ ozs. gin                    ½ slice orange
1 oz. orange juice

Shake gin and orange juice well with ice. Strain into prechilled sugar-frosted cocktail glass. Add orange slice.

## ORANGE BLOSSOM, FROZEN

1½ ozs. gin                    2 drops orange-
2 ozs. orange juice               flower water
½ oz. curaçao                  ¼ cup cracked ice
½ oz. lemon juice              ½ slice orange

Put gin, orange juice, curaçao, lemon juice, orange-flower water and ice into blender. Spin 5–8 seconds. Pour into deep-saucer champagne or old-fashioned glass. Place orange slice on top.

## PINK GIN

2 ozs. gin                     2 dashes Angostura
                                  bitters

In Britain, the custom is simply to stir these ingredients at room temperature in a small cocktail glass. For American tastes, it's more pleasant if the gin and bitters are well stirred with ice and then poured into a prechilled glass.

## PINK LADY

1½ ozs. gin                    1 teaspoon grenadine
¼ oz. lime juice               ½ egg white
1 teaspoon cream

Shake well with ice. Strain into prechilled cocktail glass. Glass may be sugar-frosted by moistening rim with grenadine before dipping into sugar.

## PIROUETTER

| | |
|---|---|
| 1   oz. gin | 1   teaspoon lemon |
| ½ oz. Grand Marnier | juice |
| 1   oz. orange juice | Orange peel |

Shake gin, Grand Marnier, orange juice and lemon juice well with ice. Strain into prechilled cocktail glass. Twist orange peel above drink and drop into glass.

## POLISH SIDECAR

| | |
|---|---|
| ¾ oz. gin | ¾ oz. Polish or |
| ¾ oz. lemon juice | Polish-style black- |
| | berry liqueur |

Shake well with ice. Strain into prechilled cocktail glass. A large fresh blackberry, if available, is a pleasant garnish for this drink.

## POMPANO

| | |
|---|---|
| 1   oz. gin | 4   dashes orange bitters |
| ½ oz. dry vermouth | 1   slice orange |
| 1   oz. grapefruit juice | |

Shake gin, vermouth, grapefruit juice and bitters well with ice. Strain over rocks in prechilled old-fashioned glass. Garnish with orange slice. A perfect cocktail for Florida- or Caribbean-bound vacationers.

## PRINCETON

| | |
|---|---|
| 1¼ ozs. gin | ½ oz. lime juice |
| ¾ oz. dry vermouth | |

Shake with ice. Strain into prechilled cocktail glass. Named for the great seat of learning which, during the Noble Experiment, distinguished itself even more for its prowess in soaking up bathtub gin.

## RED CLOUD

| | |
|---|---|
| 1½ ozs. gin | 1 teaspoon grenadine |
| ½ oz. apricot liqueur | 1 dash bitters |
| ½ oz. lemon juice | |

Shake with ice. Strain into prechilled cocktail glass.

## RENAISSANCE

| | |
|---|---|
| 1½ ozs. gin | Freshly grated |
| ½ oz. dry sherry | nutmeg |
| ½ oz. cream | |

Shake gin, sherry and cream well with ice. Strain into prechilled cocktail glass. Spray with nutmeg. A drink to savor after a lengthy tour of art galleries.

## RENDEZVOUS

| | |
|---|---|
| 1½ ozs. gin | ¼ oz. Campari |
| ½ oz. kirschwasser | Lemon peel |

Shake gin, kirschwasser and Campari well with ice. Strain into prechilled cocktail glass. Twist lemon peel above drink and drop into glass. An appetite arouser best sipped while a double-thick filet is browning over the charcoals.

## ROCKY DANE

| | |
|---|---|
| 1 oz. gin | ¼ oz. kirsch |
| ½ oz. dry vermouth | Lemon peel |
| ½ oz. Cherry Heering | |

Shake gin, vermouth, Cherry Heering and kirsch with ice. Strain over rocks in prechilled old-fashioned glass. Twist lemon peel above drink and drop into glass.

## ROSE

| | |
|---|---|
| *1  oz. gin* | *½  oz. lemon juice* |
| *½  oz. apricot-flavored* | *1  teaspoon grenadine* |
| *brandy* | *Lemon peel* |
| *½  oz. dry vermouth* | |

Shake gin, apricot-flavored brandy, vermouth, lemon juice and grenadine well with ice. Strain into prechilled cocktail glass. Twist lemon peel above drink and drop into glass.

## ST.-LO

| | |
|---|---|
| *1½  ozs. gin* | *½  oz. lemon juice* |
| *½  oz. calvados* | *1   teaspoon sugar* |

Shake well with ice. Strain into prechilled cocktail glass.

## SAN SEBASTIAN

| | |
|---|---|
| *1  oz. gin* | *¼  oz. curaçao* |
| *¼  oz. rum* | *½  oz. lemon juice* |
| *½  oz. grapefruit juice* | |

Shake well with ice. Strain into prechilled cocktail glass. Recommended for galley bartenders after a lazy Sunday-afternoon sail.

## SEVILLE

| | |
|---|---|
| *1  oz. gin* | *½  oz. lemon juice* |
| *½  oz. fino sherry* | *½  teaspoon sugar* |
| *½  oz. orange juice* | |

Shake well with ice. Strain into prechilled sugar-rimmed glass.

## SOUTH SIDE

| | |
|---|---|
| 2   ozs. gin | 1   teaspoon sugar |
| ½ oz. lemon juice | 2   sprigs fresh mint |

Shake gin, lemon juice and sugar well with ice. Strain into prechilled cocktail glass. Tear several leaves of each mint sprig before adding to drink. Although not as well known as the mint julep, the south side is a delightful cocktail with a delicate mint accent.

## STRAWBERRY SWIG

| | |
|---|---|
| 1½ ozs. gin | ¼ oz. lime juice |
| ½ oz. strawberry liqueur | 1   dash orange bitters |
| | 1   slice lime |

Shake gin, strawberry liqueur, lime juice and bitters well with ice. Strain into prechilled old-fashioned glass with several rocks. Garnish with lime slice.

## STREGA SOUR

| | |
|---|---|
| 1½ ozs. gin | ¼ oz. Strega |
| ½ oz. lemon juice | 1   slice lemon |

Shake gin, lemon juice and Strega well with ice. Strain into prechilled sugar-frosted cocktail glass. Moisten rim of glass with Strega before dipping into sugar. Garnish with lemon slice.

## TURF

| | |
|---|---|
| 1   oz. gin | ¼ oz. lemon juice |
| 1   oz. dry vermouth | 1   slice lemon |
| ¼ oz. Pernod | |

Shake gin, vermouth, Pernod and lemon juice well with ice. Strain over rocks in prechilled old-fashioned glass. Add lemon slice.

## VERBOTEN

1  oz. gin
½ oz. Forbidden
   Fruit

½ oz. lemon juice
½ oz. orange juice
1  brandied cherry

Shake gin, Forbidden Fruit, lemon juice and orange juice well with ice. Strain into prechilled cocktail glass. Garnish with brandied cherry.

## WHITE ROSE

1¼ ozs. gin
½ oz. orange juice
½ oz. lime juice

1  teaspoon sugar
½ egg white

Shake well with ice. Strain into prechilled cocktail glass. There are dozens of different recipes bearing the name white rose. This balmy concoction is designed for sipping in the vicinity of a glowing fireplace.

## WOODSTOCK

1½ ozs. gin
1  oz. lemon juice

¼ oz. maple syrup
1  dash orange bitters

Shake well with ice. Strain into frosty cocktail glass. A drink from the ski country.

# Rum Cocktails

## ACAPULCO

1¾ ozs. light rum     ½ egg white
½ oz. lime juice     ½ teaspoon sugar
¼ oz. triple sec     2 fresh mint leaves

Shake rum, lime juice, triple sec, egg white and sugar well with ice. Strain into prechilled cocktail glass. Tear each mint leaf partially and drop into glass.

## APRICOT LADY

1½ ozs. light rum     ½ teaspoon curaçao
1 oz. apricot-flavored     ½ egg white
    brandy     ¼ cup crushed ice
½ oz. lime juice     ½ slice orange

Put rum, apricot-flavored brandy, lime juice, curaçao, egg white and ice into blender. Blend 15 seconds at low speed. Pour into prechilled old-fashioned glass. Add ice cubes or ice slices to fill glass to rim. Place orange slice on top.

## APRICOT PIE

1 oz. light rum     ½ teaspoon lemon juice
1 oz. sweet vermouth     ¼ teaspoon grenadine
½ teaspoon apricot-     Orange peel
    flavored brandy

Shake rum, vermouth, apricot-flavored brandy, lemon juice and grenadine well with ice. Strain into prechilled cocktail glass. Twist orange peel above drink and drop into glass.

# BACARDI

*1½ ozs. light or*　　　*½ oz. lime juice*
　　　*golden Bacardi*　*1 teaspoon grenadine*
　　　*rum*

Shake well with ice. Strain into prechilled cocktail glass or over rocks in a prechilled old-fashioned glass.

# BANANA MANGO

*1½ ozs. light rum*　　*½ oz. lime juice*
*¼ oz. banana liqueur*　*1 slice fresh mango*
*½ oz. mango nectar*

Shake rum, banana liqueur, mango nectar and lime juice well with ice. Strain over rocks in prechilled old-fashioned glass. Add mango slice.

# BEACHCOMBER

*1½ ozs. rum*　　　*¼ teaspoon maraschino*
*½ oz. lime juice*　　　*liqueur*
*½ oz. triple sec*

Shake well with ice. Strain into prechilled sugar-rimmed cocktail glass.

# BEACHCOMBER'S GOLD

*1½ ozs. light rum*　　*½ oz. sweet vermouth*
*½ oz. dry vermouth*

Stir well with ice. Strain into prechilled deep-saucer champagne glass. Add cracked ice or ice slices to fill glass. The same mixture of rum and both kinds of vermouth is also known as the rum perfect, usually served in a regular cocktail glass without added ice. Either way, it's delightful.

## BEE'S KNEES

1½  ozs. light rum          1  teaspoon sugar
¾  oz. orange juice        2  dashes orange bitters
½  oz. lime juice             Orange peel

Shake rum, orange juice, lime juice, sugar and bitters
well with ice. Strain into prechilled cocktail glass. Twist
orange peel above drink and drop into glass. A speak-
easy heirloom whose orange accent is most mellow.

## BETWEEN THE SHEETS

¾  oz. light rum              ¾  oz. Cointreau
¾  oz. California brandy   ½  oz. lemon juice

Shake well with ice. Strain into prechilled cocktail
glass. An exhilarating variation on the rum sidecar.

## BLACK DEVIL

2  ozs. light rum            1  black olive
½  oz. dry vermouth

Stir rum and vermouth well with ice. Strain into prechilled cocktail glass. Add black olive.

## BOLERO

1½  ozs. light rum          ¼  teaspoon sweet
¾  oz. apple brandy            vermouth
                                        Lemon peel

Stir rum, apple brandy and vermouth well with ice.
Strain into prechilled sugar-frosted cocktail glass. Twist
lemon peel above drink and drop into glass.

# BOLO

1½ ozs. light rum  
½ oz. lemon juice  
½ oz. orange juice  

½ teaspoon sugar  
½ slice lemon  

Shake rum, lemon juice, orange juice and sugar well with ice. Strain into prechilled cocktail glass or prechilled whiskey-sour glass. Garnish with lemon slice.

# BORINQUEN

1½ ozs. light rum  
½ oz. passion-fruit syrup  
¾ oz. lime juice  

½ oz. orange juice  
1 teaspoon 151-proof rum  
½ cup crushed ice  

Put all ingredients into blender. Blend at low speed 10 seconds. Pour into prechilled double old-fashioned glass. Add ice cubes or cracked ice to fill glass. Garnish with gardenia if available.

# BUSHRANGER

1 oz. light rum  
1 oz. Dubonnet  

2 dashes Angostura bitters  
Lemon peel  

Shake rum, Dubonnet and bitters well with ice. Strain into prechilled cocktail glass. Twist lemon peel above drink and drop into glass.

# CARDINAL COCKTAIL I

2 ozs. light rum  
¼ oz. orzata  
1 teaspoon grenadine  

¼ oz. triple sec  
1 oz. lime juice  
1 slice lime  

Shake rum, orzata, grenadine, triple sec and lime juice well with ice. Strain into prechilled old-fashioned glass. Add ice cubes to bring liquid to rim. Garnish with lime slice.

## CARIB

| | |
|---|---|
| 1 oz. light rum | 1 teaspoon sugar |
| 1 oz. gin | 1 slice orange |
| ½ oz. lime juice | |

Shake rum, gin, lime juice and sugar well with ice. Strain over rocks in prechilled old-fashioned glass. Garnish with orange slice.

## CASA BLANCA

| | |
|---|---|
| 2 ozs. golden rum | ¼ teaspoon curaçao |
| 1 dash Angostura bitters | ¼ teaspoon maraschino liqueur |
| 1 teaspoon lime juice | |

Shake with ice. Strain into prechilled cocktail glass.

## CHERRY DAIQUIRI

| | |
|---|---|
| 1½ ozs. light rum | ¼ teaspoon kirsch |
| ½ oz. lime juice | Lime peel |
| ½ oz. tart cherry liqueur | |

Shake rum, lime juice, cherry liqueur and kirsch well with ice. Strain into prechilled cocktail glass. Twist lime peel above drink and drop into glass.

## CHINA

| | |
|---|---|
| 2 ozs. golden rum | 1 teaspoon curaçao |
| ¼ teaspoon grenadine | 1 dash Angostura bitters |
| ¼ teaspoon passion-fruit syrup | |

Mix well with ice. Pour into prechilled cocktail glass. A sweet drink, but not a dessert cocktail; one to set the mood for a roast-duck dinner.

## COLUMBIA

1½ ozs. light rum
½ oz. raspberry syrup
½ oz. lemon juice

1 teaspoon
    kirschwasser

Shake well with ice. Strain into prechilled sugar-frosted cocktail glass. The kirschwasser, though small in proportion, comes through vividly.

## CONCH SHELL

4 ozs. light rum          ½ oz. lime juice

Shake well with ice. Pour over rocks in prechilled double old-fashioned glass. Allow at least an hour for polishing this one off.

## CONTINENTAL

1¾ ozs. light rum
½ oz. lime juice
½ teaspoon sugar

½ teaspoon green
    crème de menthe

Shake well with ice. Pour into prechilled cocktail glass. A light bracer before a seafood dinner.

## CORKSCREW

1½ ozs. light rum
½ oz. dry vermouth

½ oz. peach liqueur
1 slice lime

Shake rum, vermouth and peach liqueur well with ice. Pour into prechilled cocktail glass. Add lime slice.

## CREOLE

1½ ozs. light rum
1 dash Tabasco sauce
1 teaspoon lemon
    juice

Iced beef bouillon or
    consommé (un-
    diluted)
Salt and pepper

Put two large ice cubes into prechilled old-fashioned glass. Add rum, Tabasco and lemon juice. Stir well. Fill glass with beef bouillon. Sprinkle with salt and pepper. Stir again. A pleasant pick-me-up or prebrunch cocktail.

## CUBA LIBRE COCKTAIL

1 oz. light rum
½ oz. 151-proof rum
½ oz. cola drink

½ oz. lime juice
½ teaspoon sugar
Lime peel

Shake both kinds of rum, cola drink, lime juice and sugar well with ice. Strain into prechilled cocktail glass. Twist lime peel above drink and drop into glass. Not to be confused with cuba libre, a tall rum-cola drink that's somewhat slower in its liberating effects.

## CULROSS

1½ ozs. golden rum
½ oz. Lillet

1 teaspoon apricot-
    flavored brandy
1 teaspoon lime juice

Shake well with ice. Strain into prechilled cocktail glass as a straight-up drink or over the rocks in a prechilled old-fashioned glass. Equally good either way.

## DAIQUIRI

2 ozs. light rum          ½ teaspoon sugar
½ oz. lime juice

Shake well with ice. Pour into prechilled sugar-frosted cocktail glass or over the rocks in an old-fashioned glass. Sugar may be increased for a sweeter daiquiri.

## DERBY DAIQUIRI

1½ ozs. light rum         ½ oz. simple syrup
½ oz. lime juice          ⅓ cup crushed ice
1  oz. orange juice

Put all ingredients into blender. Blend 10–15 seconds at low speed. Pour into prechilled deep-saucer champagne glass.

## DEVIL'S TAIL

1½ ozs. golden rum        ¼ oz. apricot liqueur
1  oz. vodka              ⅓ cup crushed ice
½ oz. lime juice          Lime peel
¼ oz. grenadine

Put rum, vodka, lime juice, grenadine, apricot liqueur and ice into blender. Blend at low speed 10–15 seconds. Pour into prechilled deep-saucer champagne glass. Twist lime peel above drink and drop into glass.

## EL PRESIDENTE

1½ ozs. golden rum        1  teaspoon curaçao
½ oz. dry vermouth        2  teaspoons lime juice
1  teaspoon dark          ¼ teaspoon grenadine
   Jamaican rum

Shake well with ice. Strain into prechilled cocktail glass. Hail to the chief.

## FERN GULLY

| | |
|---|---|
| 1 oz. dark Jamaican rum | ½ oz. lime juice |
| 1 oz. light rum | 2 teaspoons orange juice |
| ½ oz. cream of coconut | 1 teaspoon orzata |
| | ⅓ cup crushed ice |

Put all ingredients into blender. Blend 10–15 seconds at low speed. Pour into prechilled deep-saucer champagne glass. More rummy than the usual frozen daiquiri, but delicious.

## FT. LAUDERDALE

| | |
|---|---|
| 1½ ozs. golden rum | ¼ oz. lime juice |
| ½ oz. sweet vermouth | 1 slice cocktail orange in syrup |
| ¼ oz. orange juice | |

Shake rum, vermouth, orange juice and lime juice well with ice. Strain over rocks in prechilled old-fashioned glass. Add orange slice.

## FROSTY DAWN COCKTAIL

| | |
|---|---|
| 1½ ozs. light rum | ¼ oz. maraschino liqueur |
| 1 oz. orange juice | |
| ½ oz. Falernum | |

Shake well with ice. Pour over rocks in prechilled old-fashioned glass.

## FROZEN APPLE DAIQUIRI

| | |
|---|---|
| 1½ ozs. light rum | 1 teaspoon sugar |
| ½ oz. apple juice | 1 wedge apple, with skin |
| ½ oz. lemon juice | |
| ⅓ cup crushed ice | |

Put rum, apple juice, lemon juice, crushed ice and sugar into blender. Blend 10–15 seconds at low speed. Pour into prechilled deep-saucer champagne glass. Add apple wedge.

## FROZEN BERKELEY

1½ ozs. light rum
½ oz. California
    brandy

½ oz. passion-fruit
    syrup
½ oz. lemon juice
⅓ cup crushed ice

Put all ingredients into blender. Blend 10–15 seconds at low speed. Pour into prechilled deep-saucer champagne glass.

## FROZEN DAIQUIRI

1½ to 2 ozs. light rum
½ oz. lime juice

½ to 1 teaspoon sugar
½ cup crushed ice

Put all ingredients into blender. Blend at low speed 10–15 seconds. Pour into prechilled deep-saucer champagne glass. May be served with a small straw. The drink can be made rummier by floating a teaspoon of 151-proof rum on top, or the drink may be made with golden rum or any of the heavier-bodied rums such as Jamaican, Barbados or Martinique.

## FROZEN GUAVA DAIQUIRI

1½ ozs. light rum
1 oz. guava nectar
    (not syrup)
½ oz. lime juice

1 teaspoon banana
    liqueur
⅓ cup crushed ice

Put all ingredients into blender. Blend 10–15 seconds at low speed. Pour into prechilled deep-saucer champagne glass.

## FROZEN GUAVA-ORANGE DAIQUIRI

1½ ozs. light rum          ½ oz. orange juice
¾ oz. guava syrup          ⅓ cup crushed ice
½ oz. lime juice

Put all ingredients into blender. Blend 10–15 seconds at low speed. Pour into prechilled deep-saucer champagne glass.

## FROZEN LIME DAIQUIRI

2  ozs. light rum          ⅓ cup crushed ice
½ oz. lime liqueur         Lime peel
½ oz. lime juice

Put rum, lime liqueur, lime juice and crushed ice into blender. Blend at low speed 10–15 seconds. Pour into prechilled deep-saucer champagne glass. Twist lime peel above drink and drop into glass.

## FROZEN MANGO-LIME DAIQUIRI

1½ ozs. light rum          ½ oz. lime juice
1  oz. mango nectar        ⅓ cup crushed ice
½ oz. lime liqueur         1  slice fresh mango

Put rum, mango nectar, lime liqueur, lime juice and ice into blender. Blend at low speed 10–15 seconds. Pour into prechilled deep-saucer champagne glass. Garnish with slice of fresh mango if in season.

## FROZEN MINT DAIQUIRI

2  ozs. light rum          1  teaspoon sugar
½ oz. lime juice           ½ cup crushed ice
6  large mint leaves

Blend all ingredients in blender 20 seconds at low speed. Pour into prechilled deep-saucer champagne glass.

## FROZEN PASSION-FRUIT DAIQUIRI

1½ ozs. light rum  
½ oz. passion-fruit  
    syrup  
½ oz. lime juice  

½ oz. orange juice  
¼ oz. lemon juice  
⅓ cup crushed ice  

Put all ingredients into blender. Blend at low speed 10–15 seconds. Pour into prechilled deep-saucer champagne glass.

## FROZEN PEACH DAIQUIRI

1½ ozs. light rum  
½ oz. lime juice  
¼ cup frozen sliced  
    peaches, thawed  

½ oz. syrup from  
    frozen peaches  
⅓ cup crushed ice  

Put all ingredients into blender. Blend at low speed 10–15 seconds. Pour into prechilled deep-saucer champagne glass. You'll find the rich flavor of the frozen peaches and their syrup peachier than the fresh fruit for this drink.

## FROZEN PINEAPPLE DAIQUIRI

1½ ozs. light rum  
½ oz. lime juice  
½ teaspoon sugar  

4 canned pineapple  
    chunks, drained  
⅓ cup crushed ice  

Put all ingredients into blender. Blend 10–15 seconds at low speed. Pour into prechilled deep-saucer champagne glass. The canned pineapple is actually better than the fresh for this fruity cocktail.

## FROZEN SESAME DAIQUIRI

1½  ozs. rum
½  oz. sesame syrup
    (ajonjoli)
½  oz. lime juice

½  oz. dry vermouth
½  oz. orange juice
⅓  cup crushed ice

Put all ingredients into blender. Blend at low speed
10–15 seconds. Pour into prechilled deep-saucer champagne glass.


## FROZEN SOURSOP DAIQUIRI

1½  ozs. light rum
¼  oz. dark Jamaican
    rum
1  oz. guanabana
    (soursop) nectar

¼  oz. lime juice
¼  cup sliced banana
⅓  cup crushed ice

Put all ingredients into blender. Blend 10–15 seconds at
low speed. Pour into prechilled deep-saucer champagne
glass. The delicious soursop is now shipped to the
States as a canned nectar.


## GAUGUIN

2  ozs. light rum
½  oz. passion-fruit
    syrup
½  oz. lemon juice

¼  oz. lime juice
⅓  cup crushed ice
1  maraschino cherry

Put rum, passion-fruit syrup, lemon juice, lime juice
and ice into blender. Blend at low speed 10–15 seconds.
Pour into prechilled deep-saucer champagne glass. Add
cherry.

## GOLDEN GATE

¾ oz. light rum
¾ oz. gin
1 teaspoon 151-proof
    rum

½ oz. lemon juice
½ oz. crème de cacao
½ teaspoon Falernum
1 slice orange

Shake light rum, gin, 151-proof rum, lemon juice, crème de cacao and Falernum well with ice. Strain over rocks in a prechilled old-fashioned glass. Add orange slice. It leaves a rich afterglow.

## GUANABANA

1½ ozs. light rum
1 oz. guanabana
    (soursop) nectar

1 teaspoon lime
    juice

Shake with ice. Strain into prechilled cocktail glass.

## HURRICANE

1 oz. light rum
1 oz. golden rum
½ oz. passion-fruit
    syrup

2 teaspoons lime
    juice

Shake with ice. Strain into prechilled cocktail glass.

## ISLE OF THE BLESSED COCONUT

1½ ozs. light rum
½ oz. cream of
    coconut (canned
    coconut syrup)
½ oz. lime juice

¼ oz. lemon juice
¼ oz. orange juice
½ teaspoon sugar
⅓ cup crushed ice

Put all ingredients into blender. Blend at low speed 10–15 seconds. Pour into prechilled deep-saucer champagne glass. Serve with a bowl of toasted coconut slices.

## JADE

1¾ ozs. golden rum
½ teaspoon green
   crème de menthe
½ teaspoon curaçao

1½ teaspoons lime juice
1 teaspoon sugar
1 slice lime

Shake rum, crème de menthe, curaçao, lime juice and
sugar well with ice. Strain into prechilled cocktail glass.
Add lime slice. Minty, but not overpowering.

## LEEWARD

1½ ozs. light rum
½ oz. calvados

½ oz. sweet vermouth
Lemon peel

Shake rum, calvados and vermouth well with ice.
Strain over rocks in prechilled old-fashioned glass.
Twist lemon peel above drink and drop into glass.

## LIME DAIQUIRI

1½ ozs. light rum
½ oz. lime liqueur

½ oz. lime juice
Lime peel

Shake rum, lime liqueur and lime juice well with ice.
Strain into prechilled cocktail glass. Twist lime peel
above drink and drop into glass.

## MAI TAI

3 ozs. light rum
½ oz. lime juice
¼ teaspoon triple sec
¼ teaspoon orzata

½ teaspoon sugar
1 slice lime
1 sprig mint
1 pineapple stick

Shake rum, lime juice, triple sec, orzata and sugar
well with ice. Strain into prechilled double old-fashioned
glass. Add enough ice to fill glass. Garnish with lime
slice, mint sprig and pineapple stick.

## MANDEVILLE

1½ ozs. light rum
1 oz. dark Jamaican
   rum
¾ oz. lemon juice

1 teaspoon Pernod
½ oz. cola drink
¼ teaspoon grenadine
1 slice orange

Shake both kinds of rum, lemon juice, Pernod, cola drink and grenadine well with ice. Strain over rocks in prechilled old-fashioned glass. Add orange slice.

## MUSKMELON

1½ ozs. light rum
¼ cup sliced ripe
   cantaloupe meat
⅓ cup crushed ice
½ teaspoon sugar

½ oz. lime juice
½ oz. orange juice
1 cube cantaloupe
   meat on cocktail
   spear

Put rum, sliced cantaloupe, ice, sugar, lime juice and orange juice into blender. Blend at low speed 10–15 seconds. Pour into prechilled old-fashioned glass. Add ice cubes or ice slices, if necessary, to fill glass to rim. Garnish with cantaloupe cube.

## NAVY GROG

1 oz. dark Jamaican
   rum
½ oz. light rum
½ oz. lime juice
½ oz. orange juice

½ oz. pineapple juice
½ oz. guava nectar
¼ oz. Falernum
½ cup crushed ice
4 large mint leaves

Put both kinds of rum, lime juice, orange juice, pineapple juice, guava nectar, Falernum and crushed ice into blender. Blend at low speed 15 seconds. Pour into double old-fashioned glass. Add ice to fill glass to rim. Tear mint leaves partially and float on drink. Serve with straw.

## OCHO RIOS

1½ ozs. Jamaican rum          ½ oz. lime juice
1  oz. guava nectar            ½ teaspoon sugar
½ oz. cream                    ⅓ cup crushed ice

Put all ingredients into blender. Blend at low speed
10–15 seconds. Pour into prechilled deep-saucer champagne glass. A creamy, rummy drink recommended
after a spearfishing expedition.

## PAGO PAGO

1½ ozs. golden rum            ¼ teaspoon crème de
½ oz. fresh lime juice            cacao
½ teaspoon green              ½ oz. pineapple juice
    Chartreuse

Shake well with ice. Strain into prechilled cocktail
glass. Pineapple comes through beautifully.

## PENSACOLA

1½ ozs. light rum             ½ oz. lemon juice
½ oz. guava nectar            ⅓ cup crushed ice
½ oz. orange juice

Put all ingredients into blender. Blend 10–15 seconds
at low speed. Pour into prechilled deep-saucer champagne glass.

## PINK CREOLE

1½ ozs. golden rum            1  teaspoon grenadine
½ oz. lime juice              1  black cherry, soaked
1  teaspoon cream                in rum

Shake rum, lime juice, cream and grenadine well with
ice. Strain into prechilled cocktail glass. Add cherry.

## PINK VERANDA

1 oz. golden rum
½ oz. heavy Jamaican
    rum
1½ ozs. cranberry juice

½ oz. lime juice
1 teaspoon sugar
½ egg white

Shake well with ice. Strain into prechilled old-fashioned glass. Add ice, if necessary, to fill glass to rim.

## POLYNESIA

1½ ozs. light rum
1 oz. passion-fruit
    syrup

¼ oz. lime juice
½ egg white
⅓ cup crushed ice

Put all ingredients into blender. Blend 10–15 seconds at low speed. Pour into prechilled deep-saucer champagne glass.

## POLYNESIAN PARADISE

1½ ozs. golden rum
1 teaspoon brown
    sugar
¾ oz. lime juice

½ oz. sweet vermouth
¼ oz. triple sec
⅓ cup crushed ice

Put all ingredients into blender. Blend at low speed 10–15 seconds. Pour into prechilled deep-saucer champagne glass. Paradise enow.

## PONCE DE LEON

1½ ozs. light rum
½ oz. grapefruit juice
½ oz. mango nectar

1 teaspoon lemon
    juice

Shake well with ice. Strain into prechilled sugar-frosted cocktail glass.

## PORT ANTONIO

1  oz. golden rum
½ oz. dark Jamaican
    rum
½ oz. lime juice

½ oz. coffee liqueur
1  teaspoon Falernum
1  slice lime

Shake both kinds of rum, lime juice, coffee liqueur and Falernum well with ice. Strain over rocks in pre-chilled old-fashioned glass. Add lime slice.

## PORT MARIA

1½ ozs. light rum
¾ oz. pineapple juice
½ oz. lemon juice

1  teaspoon Falernum
   Grated nutmeg

Shake liquids well with ice. Strain into prechilled cocktail glass. Sprinkle nutmeg on top.

## PUERTO RICAN PINK LADY

1½ ozs. golden rum
¾ oz. lemon juice
½ egg white

1  teaspoon grenadine
⅓ cup crushed ice

Put all ingredients into blender. Blend at low speed 10–15 seconds. Pour into prechilled sugar-rimmed deep-saucer champagne glass.

## ROSE HALL

1  oz. dark Jamaican
    rum
1  oz. orange juice
½ oz. banana liqueur

1  teaspoon lime
    juice
1  slice lime

Shake rum, orange juice, banana liqueur and lime juice well with ice. Strain over rocks in prechilled old-fashioned glass. Add lime slice.

## RUM AND SHERRY

1½ ozs. light rum          1   maraschino cherry
¾ oz. sherry

Stir rum and sherry well with ice. Strain into pre-chilled cocktail glass. The felicitous blend of rum and sherry may be made with very dry cocktail sherry, medium amontillado or rich cream sherry to meet your own choice of dryness or sweetness. All are good.

## RUM DUBONNET

1½ ozs. light rum          1   teaspoon lime juice
¾ oz. Dubonnet                 Lime peel

Shake rum, Dubonnet and lime juice well with ice. Strain into prechilled cocktail glass. Twist lime peel above drink and drop into glass.

## RUM OLD-FASHIONED

½ teaspoon sugar           2   ozs. light, golden
1   or 2 dashes                or dark Jamaican
      Angostura bitters        rum
1   teaspoon water             Lime peel
                           1   teaspoon 151-proof
                               rum

Mix sugar, bitters and water in old-fashioned glass until sugar is completely dissolved. Add two ice cubes or several pieces of cracked ice. Add 2 ozs. rum. Stir well. Twist lime peel above drink and drop into glass. Float 151-proof rum on top.

## RUM SCREWDRIVER

1½ ozs. light rum          1  slice orange
 3  ozs. cold fresh
      orange juice

Put rum and orange juice (without ice) into blender.
Blend 10–15 seconds at low speed. Pour over rocks
in old-fashioned glass. Garnish with orange slice. A
drink sometimes known as the Aunt Agatha, though it's
the most un–Aunt Agathaish drink we can imagine.

## RUM SOUR

2  ozs. light or golden     1  teaspoon rock-candy
      rum                        syrup or sugar
½ oz. lemon juice          ½ slice lemon
1  teaspoon orange
      juice

Shake rum, lemon juice, orange juice and syrup or
sugar well with ice. Strain into prechilled whiskey-
sour glass. Add lemon slice. A teaspoon of 151-proof
rum may be floated on top for a more rummish accent.

## SAGUENAY

1  oz. light rum           2  teaspoons crème de
1  oz. dry vermouth             cassis
1  teaspoon lemon
      juice

Shake well with ice. Strain over rocks in prechilled
old-fashioned glass.

## ST. AUGUSTINE

1½ ozs. light rum          1  teaspoon Cointreau
 1  oz. grapefruit juice       Lemon peel

Shake rum, grapefruit juice and Cointreau well with ice. Strain into prechilled sugar-rimmed cocktail glass. Twist lemon peel above drink and drop into glass. Perfect before a pompano dinner.

## SAN JUAN

1½ ozs. rum
1 oz. grapefruit juice
1 teaspoon cream of
    coconut
2 teaspoons lime juice
⅓ cup crushed ice
2 teaspoons 151-proof
    rum

Put 1½ ozs. rum, grapefruit juice, cream of coconut, lime juice and ice into blender. Blend at low speed 10–15 seconds. Pour into prechilled deep-saucer champagne glass. Float 151-proof rum on top.

## SCORPION

2 ozs. light rum
2 ozs. orange juice
1½ ozs. lemon juice
1 oz. California
    brandy
½ oz. orzata
⅓ cup crushed ice
1 slice orange

Put rum, orange juice, lemon juice, brandy, orzata and ice into blender. Blend at low speed 10–15 seconds. Pour into prechilled double old-fashioned glass with enough ice cubes to fill glass to rim. Add orange slice.

## SEPTEMBER MORN

1½ ozs. light rum
½ oz. lime juice
1 teaspoon grenadine
½ egg white

Shake well with ice. Strain into prechilled sugar-frosted cocktail glass. Glass rim may be moistened with grenadine before dipping into sugar.

## SESAME

1½ ozs. light rum      ½ oz. sesame-seed
½ oz. lime juice         syrup (ajonjoli)

Shake well with ice. Strain into prechilled cocktail glass. Sesame is a versatile seed. It's available in syrup form in stores featuring Caribbean products.

## SHARK'S TOOTH

1½ ozs. golden rum     ¼ oz. sloe gin
¼ oz. lemon juice      1   dash Angostura
¼ oz. passion-fruit       bitters
    syrup            Orange peel
¼ oz. sweet vermouth   1   maraschino cherry

Shake rum, lemon juice, passion-fruit syrup, vermouth, sloe gin and bitters well with ice. Strain into prechilled sugar-frosted cocktail glass. Twist orange peel above drink and drop into glass. Add cherry.

## SOUTHERN BANANA COMFORT

1 oz. golden rum      ½ oz. lime juice
1 oz. Southern        1 teaspoon sugar
    Comfort         ⅓ cup crushed ice
¼ cup sliced banana

Put ingredients into blender. Blend at low speed 10–15 seconds. Pour into prechilled saucer champagne glass.

## STRATOSPHERE

1 oz. rum           ¼ oz. tart cherry
½ oz. California       liqueur
    brandy          ½ oz. lemon juice
                    1 teaspoon sugar

Shake with ice. Strain into prechilled cocktail glass.

# TAHITI CLUB

2  ozs. golden rum
½  oz. lime juice
½  oz. pineapple juice
½  oz. lemon juice

½  teaspoon maraschino
   liqueur
1  slice orange

Shake rum, lime juice, pineapple juice, lemon juice and maraschino liqueur well with ice. Strain into pre-chilled old-fashioned glass. Add cracked ice or ice cubes to fill glass. Add orange slice.

# TOBAGO

1  oz. golden rum
1  oz. gin
1  teaspoon 151-proof
   rum
2  teaspoons lime juice

1  teaspoon guava
   syrup (not nectar)
⅓  cup crushed ice
   Lime peel

Put golden rum, gin, 151-proof rum, lime juice, guava syrup and ice into blender. Blend at low speed 10–15 seconds. Pour over rocks in prechilled old-fashioned glass. Twist lime peel above drink and drop into glass.

# TORRIDORA COCKTAIL

1½ ozs. light rum
½  oz. coffee liqueur
¼  oz. sweet cream

1  teaspoon 151-proof
   rum

Shake light rum, coffee liqueur and cream well with ice. Strain into prechilled cocktail glass. Float 151-proof rum on top. In the Caribbean, the dinner hour commences rather late, about nine o'clock in the evening. By this time, the sweetness of the cocktail hour will have passed on, and one will be left with a rummy repose and a fine appetite.

## TRADE WINDS

2   ozs. golden rum        1½  teaspoons sugar
½  oz. lime juice          ⅓  cup crushed ice
½  oz. plum brandy

Put all ingredients into blender. Blend at low speed
10–15 seconds. Pour into prechilled deep-saucer champagne glass. Potent with plum flavor but not a scalp
raiser.

## UNISPHERE

1½ ozs. golden rum        ½  teaspoon Benedictine
1   teaspoon grenadine    ½  teaspoon Pernod
½  oz. lime juice

Shake well with ice. Strain into prechilled cocktail
glass. Small amounts of liqueurs come through beautifully without overpowering flavor.

# Tequila Cocktails

## BLOODY MARIA

1 oz. tequila
2 ozs. ice-cold tomato
   juice
1 teaspoon lemon
   juice

1 dash Tabasco sauce
1 dash celery salt
1 slice lemon

Pour tequila, tomato juice, lemon juice, Tabasco and celery salt into prechilled old-fashioned glass. Add rocks or ice slices to fill glass. Stir very well. Add lemon slice. Viva Maria!

## BUNNY BONANZA

1½ ozs. tequila
1 oz. apple brandy
½ oz. lemon juice

1 teaspoon sugar
½ teaspoon curaçao
1 slice lemon

Shake tequila, apple brandy, lemon juice, sugar and curaçao well with ice. Strain into prechilled old-fashioned glass. Add ice to fill glass. Garnish with lemon slice, as served in the Detroit Playboy Club.

## CHAPALA

1½ ozs. tequila
½ oz. orange juice
½ oz. lemon juice

1 dash orange-
   flower water
2 teaspoons grenadine
1 slice orange

Shake tequila, orange juice, lemon juice, orange-flower water and grenadine well with ice. Strain over rocks in prechilled old-fashioned glass. Add orange slice.

## COCONUT TEQUILA

1½ ozs. tequila
½ oz. cream of
   coconut
½ oz. lemon juice

1 teaspoon maraschino
   liqueur
½ cup crushed ice

Put all ingredients into blender. Blend 20 seconds at low speed. Pour into prechilled deep-saucer champagne glass. Perfect before a Polynesian brunch.

## FROZEN BLACKBERRY TEQUILA

1½ ozs. tequila
1 oz. blackberry
   liqueur

½ oz. lemon juice
⅓ cup crushed ice
1 slice lemon

Put tequila, blackberry liqueur, lemon juice and crushed ice into blender. Blend 10–15 seconds at low speed. Pour into prechilled old-fashioned glass. Add rocks to fill glass. Add lemon slice.

## FROZEN MATADOR

1 oz. tequila
2 ozs. pineapple juice
½ oz. lime juice

⅓ cup crushed ice
1 cocktail pineapple
   stick

Put tequila, pineapple juice, lime juice and crushed ice into blender. Blend at low speed 10–15 seconds. Pour into prechilled deep-saucer champagne glass. Add pineapple stick. Or pour over rocks in prechilled old-fashioned glass. Add ice cubes to fill glass. Garnish with pineapple stick.

## MARGARITA

1½ ozs. tequila
½ oz. triple sec or
   curaçao

½ oz. lemon or lime
   juice

Shake well with ice. Strain into prechilled salt-rimmed cocktail glass. To prepare glass, rub rim with outside of lemon peel; then dip into salt and shake off excess. Although traditionally the glass for a margarita is salt-rimmed, it may also be sugar-rimmed. A twist of lime or lemon peel may be added if desired.

## MEXICO PACIFICO

1½ ozs. tequila
½ oz. lime juice
1 oz. passion-fruit
   syrup
⅓ cup crushed ice
1 slice lime

Put tequila, lime juice, passion-fruit syrup and crushed ice into blender. Blend 10–15 seconds at low speed. Pour into prechilled deep-saucer champagne glass. Add lime slice. *Exotico!*

## MINT TEQUILA

1½ ozs. tequila
6 large mint leaves
½ oz. lemon juice
1 teaspoon sugar
½ cup crushed ice

Put all ingredients into blender. Blend at low speed 15–20 seconds. Pour into prechilled old-fashioned glass. Add a rock or two to fill glass to rim.

## PRADO

1½ ozs. tequila
¾ oz. lime juice
½ egg white
½ oz. maraschino
   liqueur
1 teaspoon grenadine
½ slice lemon
1 maraschino cherry

Shake tequila, lime juice, egg white, maraschino liqueur and grenadine well with ice. Strain into prechilled whiskey-sour glass. Add lemon slice and cherry.

## SLOE TEQUILA

| | |
|---|---|
| 1 oz. tequila | ½ cup crushed ice |
| ½ oz. sloe gin | Cucumber peel |
| ½ oz. lime juice | |

Put tequila, sloe gin, lime juice and ice into blender. Blend 10–15 seconds at low speed. Pour into pre-chilled old-fashioned glass. Add cucumber peel and fill glass with cubed or cracked ice.

## SUNSET

| | |
|---|---|
| 1½ ozs. tequila | ½ cup crushed ice |
| ½ oz. lime juice | 1 slice lime |
| ½ oz. grenadine | |

Put tequila, lime juice, grenadine and ice into blender. Blend at low speed 10–15 seconds. Pour into pre-chilled old-fashioned glass. Add ice slices or cubes to fill glass. Garnish with lime slice.

## TEQUILA DUBONNET

| | |
|---|---|
| 1 oz. tequila | 1 slice lemon |
| 1 oz. Dubonnet | |

Pour tequila and Dubonnet into prechilled old-fashioned glass. Add cubed or cracked ice to fill glass. Stir. Garnish with lemon slice.

## TEQUILA FRESA

| | |
|---|---|
| 1½ ozs. tequila | ¼ teaspoon orange |
| ¾ oz. strawberry | bitters |
| liqueur | 1 slice lime |
| ½ oz. lime juice | 1 fresh strawberry |

Shake tequila, strawberry liqueur, lime juice and bitters well with ice. Strain over rocks in old-fashioned glass. Add lime slice and strawberry.

# TEQUILA FROZEN SCREWDRIVER

1½ ozs. tequila
3 ozs. iced orange
   juice

⅓ cup crushed ice
1 slice orange

Put tequila, orange juice and crushed ice into blender. Blend at low speed 10–15 seconds. Pour into prechilled old-fashioned glass. Add orange slice.

# TEQUILA GUAYABA

1½ ozs. tequila
½ oz. guava syrup
½ oz. orange juice

½ oz. lime juice
Orange peel

Shake tequila, guava syrup, orange juice and lime juice well with ice. Pour into prechilled old-fashioned glass. Add a rock or two to fill glass. Twist orange peel above drink and drop into glass. Pass a guacamole dip.

# TEQUILA OLD-FASHIONED

½ teaspoon sugar
2 dashes Angostura
   bitters
1½ ozs. tequila

Iced club soda
Lemon peel
1 cocktail pineapple
   stick

Stir sugar, bitters and 1 teaspoon water in prechilled old-fashioned glass until sugar is dissolved. Add tequila. Add rocks or cracked ice to glass. Stir well. Add a splash of soda and stir. Twist lemon peel above drink and drop into glass. Garnish with pineapple stick.

## TEQUILA SOUR

| | |
|---|---|
| 2 ozs. tequila | ½ slice lemon |
| ½ oz. lemon juice | 1 maraschino cherry |
| 1 teaspoon sugar | |

Shake tequila, lemon juice and sugar well with ice. Strain into prechilled whiskey-sour glass. Add lemon slice and cherry.

## TEQUINI

| | |
|---|---|
| 1½ to 2 ozs. tequila | 1 cocktail olive |
| ½ oz. dry vermouth | (optional) |
| Lemon peel | |

Stir tequila and vermouth well with ice. Strain into prechilled cocktail glass. Twist lemon peel above drink and drop into glass. A Mexican martini. Olive may be added for a salty accent.

# Vodka Cocktails

## AQUEDUCT

1½ ozs. vodka                 ½ oz. lime juice
¼ oz. curaçao                 Orange peel
¼ oz. apricot liqueur

Shake vodka, curaçao, apricot liqueur and lime juice
well with ice. Strain into prechilled cocktail glass.
Twist orange peel above drink and drop into glass.
Make book on this drink without any qualms.

## BLACK RUSSIAN

1½ ozs. vodka                 ¾ oz. Kahlúa coffee
                                  liqueur

Shake well with ice. Strain over rocks in prechilled
old-fashioned glass.

## BLOODY MARY

1½ ozs. vodka                 1  dash Worcestershire
3  ozs. tomato juice             sauce
½ oz. lemon juice             1  dash celery salt
1  teaspoon catsup            1  dash Tabasco sauce

Shake all ingredients well with ice. Strain into tall or
squat 8-oz. glass.

## BULL SHOT

4  ozs. chilled beef          1½ ozs. vodka
      consommé                1  slice lemon

Pour consommé and vodka over rocks in 8-oz. glass.
Stir. Add lemon slice.

## CHERRY VODKA

1½ ozs. 100-proof
    vodka
½ oz. lime juice

½ oz. Cherry Heering
    or Cherry Karise

Shake well with ice until the shaker is almost too cold to hold. Strain into prechilled cocktail glass.

## CHIQUITA

1½ ozs. vodka
½ oz. banana liqueur
¼ cup sliced ripe
    banana

½ oz. lime juice
1 teaspoon sugar
¼ cup finely crushed
    ice

Put all ingredients into blender. Spin at low speed for 15 seconds. Pour into deep-saucer champagne glass.

## FLYING GRASSHOPPER

1 oz. vodka
½ oz. green crème de
    menthe

½ oz. white crème de
    cacao

Stir well with ice. Strain into prechilled cocktail glass.

## FROZEN RUSSIAN APPLE

1½ ozs. vodka
¼ oz. calvados or
    applejack
½ oz. lime juice

¼ cup diced fresh
    apple
¼ cup finely crushed
    ice
½ teaspoon sugar

Put all ingredients into blender. Spin at low speed for 15 seconds. Pour into deep-saucer champagne glass. A north-country version of the frozen daiquiri.

## GYPSY

2  ozs. vodka
½ oz. Benedictine
1  teaspoon lemon
     juice

1  teaspoon orange
     juice
1  slice orange

Shake vodka, Benedictine, lemon juice and orange juice well with ice. Strain over rocks in prechilled old-fashioned glass. Add orange slice.

## KREMLIN COLONEL

2  ozs. vodka
½ oz. lime juice
1  teaspoon sugar

2  large fresh mint
     leaves

Shake vodka, lime juice and sugar well with ice. Strain into prechilled cocktail glass. Tear each mint leaf in half to release aroma and drop into glass.

## KRETCHMA

1  oz. vodka
1  oz. crème de cacao

½ oz. lemon juice
½ teaspoon grenadine

Shake with ice. Strain into prechilled cocktail glass.

## LORENZO

1  oz. vodka
1  oz. Tuaca liqueur

½ oz. lime juice

Shake well with ice. Strain into prechilled sugar-frosted cocktail glass. Rim of glass may be moistened with Tuaca before dipping into sugar. One sip of this and you'll understand why Lorenzo de' Medici was called El Magnifico.

## RED APPLE

| | |
|---|---|
| 1   oz. 100-proof<br>    vodka | ½  oz. lemon juice |
| 1   oz. apple juice | ½  teaspoon grenadine |
| | 1   dash orange bitters |

Shake well with ice. Strain into prechilled cocktail glass. Not to be confused with a vodka and apple juice, a lowball rather than a cocktail.

## RUSSIAN BEAR

| | |
|---|---|
| 1   oz. vodka | ½  oz. cream |
| ½  oz. crème de cacao | |

Shake well with ice. Strain into prechilled cocktail glass.

## RUSSIAN ESPRESSO

| | |
|---|---|
| 1½  ozs. vodka | ½  teaspoon lemon |
| ½  oz. espresso-coffee<br>    liqueur |     juice |
| | Lemon peel |

Pour vodka, coffee liqueur and lemon juice over rocks in prechilled old-fashioned glass. Stir well. Twist lemon peel above drink and drop into glass. A coexistence cocktail.

## SALTY DOG

| | |
|---|---|
| 2   ozs. vodka | 1   teaspoon lemon |
| ½  oz. unsweetened<br>    grapefruit juice |     juice |
| | Salt |

Shake vodka, grapefruit juice and lemon juice well with ice. Strain into prechilled cocktail glass. Sprinkle drink with several generous dashes of salt.

## SCREWDRIVER

1½ ozs. vodka
4½ ozs. ice-cold orange
   juice, freshly
   squeezed

1 teaspoon lemon
   juice (optional)

Shake extremely well with ice or pour into blender and blend with ice at high speed for 5 seconds. Strain into prechilled tall or squat 10-oz. glass.

## SOVIET

1½ ozs. vodka
½ oz. amontillado
   sherry

½ oz. dry vermouth
Lemon peel

Stir vodka, sherry and vermouth well with ice. Strain over rocks in prechilled old-fashioned glass. Twist lemon peel above drink and drop into glass.

## SVETLANA

1½ ozs. 100-proof
   vodka
½ oz. sweet vermouth

¼ oz. kirsch
¼ oz. orange juice
Orange peel

Shake vodka, vermouth, kirsch and orange juice well with ice. Strain into prechilled cocktail glass. Twist orange peel above drink and drop into glass. Serve biting cold. No *nyets* will be heard.

## TOVARICH

1½ ozs. vodka
½ oz. kümmel

½ oz. lime juice
Lime peel

Shake vodka, kümmel and lime juice well with ice. Strain into prechilled cocktail glass. Twist lime peel above drink and drop into glass.

## VODKA FRAISE

¾ oz. vodka
¾ oz. light rum
½ oz. strawberry
    liqueur

½ oz. lime juice
½ teaspoon grenadine
½ large fresh
    strawberry

Shake vodka, rum, strawberry liqueur, lime juice and grenadine well with ice. Strain into prechilled sugar-frosted cocktail glass. Float strawberry on top.

## VODKA GIMLET

2  ozs. vodka
½ oz. Rose's lime juice

Stir well with ice. Strain into prechilled cocktail glass.

## VODKA GRAND MARNIER

1½ ozs. vodka
½ oz. Grand Marnier

½ oz. lime juice
1  slice orange

Shake vodka, Grand Marnier and lime juice well with ice. Strain over rocks in prechilled old-fashioned glass. Garnish with orange slice.

## VODKA MARTINI

2¼ ozs. vodka
¼ oz. dry vermouth

Stir well with ice. Strain into prechilled cocktail glass or serve over rocks. Garnish with twist of lemon peel or olive. Lacks the zip of the gin-based martini, but is wonderful midday solace for vodka partisans.

## VODKA OLD-FASHIONED

½ teaspoon sugar
2  dashes Angostura
    bitters

½ oz. water
2  ozs. vodka
    Lemon peel

Dissolve sugar with bitters and water in old-fashioned glass. Add vodka. Fill glass to rim with cubes, slices or coarsely cracked pieces of ice. Stir very well. Twist lemon peel above drink and drop into glass.


## VODKA SOUR

1¾ ozs. vodka  
¾ oz. lemon juice  
1 teaspoon sugar  

1 slice lemon  
1 maraschino cherry  

Shake vodka, lemon juice and sugar well with ice. Strain into prechilled whiskey-sour glass. Garnish with lemon slice and cherry.


## VODKA STINGER

1½ ozs. vodka  

1½ ozs. white crème de menthe  

Shake extremely well with ice. Pour into prechilled cocktail glass. Drink must be extremely cold. May be pre- or postprandial.


## WARSAW

1½ ozs. vodka  
½ oz. blackberry liqueur  
½ oz. dry vermouth  

1 teaspoon lemon juice  
Lemon peel  

Shake vodka, blackberry liqueur, vermouth and lemon juice well with ice. Strain into prechilled cocktail glass. Twist lemon peel above drink and drop into glass. The Poles are famed for their tart blackberry liqueur, and if you can get your hands on it or on the Leroux domestic blackberry liqueur called Likier Smaku, you'll really bring the warsaw to life.

# Whiskey Cocktails

## ALLEGHENY

| | |
|---|---|
| 1 oz. bourbon | ¼ oz. lemon juice |
| 1 oz. dry vermouth | 1 dash Angostura |
| ¼ oz. blackberry | bitters |
| liqueur | Lemon peel |

Shake bourbon, vermouth, blackberry liqueur, lemon juice and bitters well with ice. Strain into prechilled cocktail glass. Twist lemon peel above drink and drop into glass.

## BLACK HAWK

| | |
|---|---|
| 1 oz. blended whiskey | ½ oz. lemon juice |
| 1 oz. sloe gin (creamy | 1 maraschino cherry |
| cap) | (optional) |

Shake whiskey, sloe gin and lemon juice well with ice. Strain into prechilled cocktail glass. Garnish with cherry.

## BOURBONNAISE

| | |
|---|---|
| 1½ ozs. bourbon | ¼ oz. crème de cassis |
| ½ oz. dry vermouth | ¼ oz. lemon juice |

Shake well with ice. Strain over rocks in prechilled old-fashioned glass. A perfect way to introduce a French girl to American bourbon.

# CANADIAN APPLE

1½ ozs. Canadian
    whisky
½ oz. calvados
¼ oz. lemon juice

1 teaspoon sugar
  Ground cinnamon
1 slice lemon

Shake whisky, calvados, lemon juice, sugar and a spray of cinnamon well with ice. Strain over rocks in pre-chilled old-fashioned glass. Add lemon slice.

# CANADIAN CHERRY

1½ ozs. Canadian
    whisky
½ oz. Cherry Heering
    or Cherry Karise

¼ oz. lemon juice
¼ oz. orange juice

Shake well with ice. Strain into prechilled sugar-frosted cocktail glass. Glass rim may be moistened with cherry liqueur before dipping into sugar.

# CANADIAN COCKTAIL

1½ ozs. Canadian
    whisky
½ oz. lemon juice

¼ oz. curaçao
1 teaspoon sugar
2 dashes bitters

Shake well with ice. Strain into prechilled cocktail glass or over rocks in old-fashioned glass.

# CANADIAN OLD-FASHIONED

1½ ozs. Canadian
    whisky
2 dashes Angostura
    bitters

½ teaspoon curaçao
½ teaspoon lemon juice
  Lemon peel
  Orange peel

Pour whisky, bitters, curaçao and lemon juice into pre-chilled old-fashioned glass. Add rocks. Stir. Twist lemon peel and orange peel above drink and drop into glass.

## CANADIAN PINEAPPLE

1½  ozs. Canadian           ½  teaspoon maraschino
       whisky                        liqueur
½  oz. pineapple juice      1  cocktail pineapple
½  oz. lemon juice              stick

Shake whisky, pineapple juice, lemon juice and maraschino liqueur well with ice. Strain over rocks in
prechilled old-fashioned glass. Add pineapple stick.

## CHAPEL HILL

1½  ozs. blended whiskey    1  slice cocktail orange
½  oz. curaçao                    in syrup
½  oz. lemon juice

Shake whiskey, curaçao and lemon juice well with ice.
Strain over rocks in prechilled old-fashioned glass.
Garnish with orange slice.

## COMMODORE

1¾  ozs. blended whiskey    1  teaspoon strawberry
 2  teaspoons lime juice           liqueur
 1  teaspoon orange juice    1  dash orange bitters

Shake well with ice. Strain into prechilled cocktail
glass.

## COMMONWEALTH

1¾  ozs. Canadian           ½  oz. Van der Hum
       whisky                        liqueur
¼  oz. lemon juice          Tangerine peel or
                                     orange peel

Shake whisky, lemon juice and Van der Hum well with
ice. Strain into prechilled sug r-frosted cocktail glass.
Twist tangerine peel above drink and drop into glass.

# CROTON

*1¾ ozs. bourbon or*      *¾ oz. cocktail sherry*
   *blended whiskey*        *Lemon peel*

Stir whiskey and sherry well with ice. Strain into prechilled cocktail glass. Twist lemon peel above drink
and drop into glass. A patio or terrace cocktail to be
served with a bowl of fresh iced shrimp and a tangy
cocktail sauce.

# CURRIER

*1½ ozs. blended whiskey*    *¼ oz. Rose's lime juice*
  *½ oz. kümmel*           *1 slice lime*
  *¼ oz. fresh lime juice*

Shake whiskey, kümmel and both kinds of lime juice
well with ice. Strain into prechilled cocktail glass. Add
lime slice. A cocktail to savor between the fox hunt
and breakfast.

# DELTA

*1½ ozs. blended whiskey*    *½ teaspoon sugar*
  *½ oz. Southern Comfort*   *½ slice orange*
  *½ oz. lime juice*        *1 slice fresh peach*

Shake whiskey, Southern Comfort, lime juice and
sugar well with ice. Strain over rocks in prechilled old-
fashioned glass. Garnish with orange and peach slices.
A drink to accompany Gershwin on the hi-fi.

# GLASGOW

*1½ ozs. Scotch whisky*     *¼ oz. dry vermouth*
  *¾ oz. lemon juice*       *¼ oz. orzata*

Shake well with ice. Strain into prechilled cocktail glass.
Serve with thin slices of Nova Scotia salmon on hot
buttered toast.

## HABITANT COCKTAIL

| | |
|---|---|
| 1½ ozs. blended Canadian whisky | 1 teaspoon maple-sugar syrup |
| 1 oz. lemon juice | 1 slice orange |
| | 1 maraschino cherry |

Shake whisky, lemon juice and syrup well with ice. Strain into prechilled old-fashioned glass. Add ice to fill glass. Garnish with orange slice and cherry, as served in the Montreal Playboy Club.

## INDIAN RIVER

| | |
|---|---|
| 1½ ozs. blended whiskey | ¼ oz. raspberry liqueur |
| ½ oz. unsweetened grapefruit juice | ¼ oz. sweet vermouth |

Shake well with ice. Strain over rocks in prechilled old-fashioned glass.

## KENTUCKY

| | |
|---|---|
| 1½ ozs. 86-proof bourbon | ½ oz. pineapple juice |
| ½ oz. lemon juice | 1 teaspoon maraschino liqueur |

Shake well with ice. Strain into prechilled sugar-frosted cocktail glass.

## LAWHILL

| | |
|---|---|
| 1½ ozs. blended whiskey | ½ oz. orange juice |
| ¾ oz. dry vermouth | 1 dash Angostura bitters |
| ¼ teaspoon Pernod | |
| ¼ teaspoon maraschino liqueur | |

Shake well with ice. Strain into prechilled cocktail glass. A superb cocktail to mix beforehand, strain into a thermos and tote along on a picnic.

## MANHASSET

1½  ozs. blended whiskey        ¼  oz. sweet vermouth
½  oz. lemon juice              Lemon peel
¼  oz. dry vermouth

Shake whiskey, lemon juice and both kinds of vermouth
well with ice. Strain into prechilled cocktail glass. Twist
lemon peel above drink and drop into glass.

## MANHATTAN

In the national drink derby two or three cocktail
generations ago, the manhattan and the martini always
wound up in a dead heat. At the present time, the
manhattan occupies the second spot. Manhattanites,
though less demanding than martini fans, have nevertheless stirred up many spirited variations on the whis-
key-vermouth theme. In public pouring houses, the
usual manhattan is made with 1½ ounces of whiskey.
At private bars, a more generous allowance of whiskey
is likely. Here's what most manhattanites expect:

1½  to 2 ozs. blended      1  dash bitters (optional)
     whiskey               1  maraschino cherry
½  oz. sweet vermouth

Stir whiskey, vermouth and bitters well with ice. Strain
into prechilled cocktail glass. Add cherry.

*Dry Manhattan:* Use dry instead of sweet vermouth;
a twist of lemon peel or an olive may be substituted
for the cherry.

*Bourbon Manhattan:* Use 86- or 100-proof bourbon
instead of blended whiskey.

*Canadian Manhattan:* Use Canadian instead of U.S.
blended whiskey; don't overstir or the delicate flavor
of the Canadian spirits will become pallid.

## MAY COCKTAIL

1½ ozs. blended whiskey     Chilled May wine
¼ oz. kirschwasser     1   slice lemon
¼ oz. strawberry liqueur

Shake whiskey, kirschwasser and strawberry liqueur
well with ice. Strain into prechilled old-fashioned glass
with a large ice cube. Fill glass with May wine. Stir.
Garnish with lemon slice.

## NEVINS

1½ ozs. bourbon     ¼ oz. lemon juice
½ oz. grapefruit juice     1   dash Angostura
¼ oz. apricot liqueur       bitters

Shake well with ice. Strain into prechilled sugar-frosted
cocktail glass.

## NEW WORLD

1¾ ozs. blended whiskey     1   teaspoon grenadine
½ oz. lime juice       Lime peel

Shake whiskey, lime juice and grenadine well with ice.
Strain into prechilled cocktail glass. Twist lime peel
above drink and drop into glass. Drink this one while
listening to Dvořák before a midnight supper.

## NEW YORK SOUR

2 ozs. blended whiskey     Chilled dry red wine
½ oz. lemon juice     ½ slice lemon
1 teaspoon sugar

Shake whiskey, lemon juice and sugar well with ice.
Strain into prechilled 6-oz. sour glass. Fill glass with
dry red wine. Stir. Garnish with lemon slice.

## NEW YORKER

1½ ozs. blended whiskey
½ oz. lime juice
1 teaspoon sugar

¼ teaspoon grenadine
Lemon peel
Orange peel

Shake whiskey, lime juice, sugar and grenadine well with ice. Strain into prechilled sugar-frosted cocktail glass. Twist lemon peel and orange peel above drink and drop into glass. A fruity terrace cocktail appreciated equally under sun or stars.

## NIGHT SHADE

1½ ozs. bourbon
½ oz. sweet vermouth
½ oz. orange juice

¼ teaspoon yellow
    Chartreuse
½ slice orange
½ slice lemon

Shake bourbon, vermouth, orange juice and Chartreuse well with ice. Strain over rocks in prechilled old-fashioned glass. Add orange and lemon slices. Pass freshly fried, generously salted shrimp chips.

## OLD-FASHIONED

½ teaspoon sugar
1 or 2 dashes Angos-
    tura bitters
2 teaspoons water or
    club soda

1½ to 2 ozs. blended
    whiskey
Lemon peel

Stir sugar, bitters and water in prechilled old-fashioned glass until sugar dissolves. Fill glass with ice cubes or large pieces of cracked ice. Add whiskey. Stir well. Twist lemon peel above drink and drop into glass. An old-fashioned may be made with U.S. blended whiskey, Canadian, Irish or Scotch. In smart men's clubs, the words *garnish* and *garbage* were once synonymous;

orange and lemon slices, cherries, cocktail sticks, etc., were considered female diversions for filling a glass with fruit instead of the cocktail itself. Over the years, this attitude has been somewhat mitigated. Generally, however, most men and women appreciate the old-fashioned unencumbered with superfluous fruit.

## PRINCE EDWARD

| | |
|---|---|
| 1¾ ozs. Scotch whisky | 1 slice cocktail orange |
| ½ oz. Lillet | in syrup |
| ¼ oz. Drambuie | |

Shake Scotch, Lillet and Drambuie well with ice. Strain over rocks in prechilled old-fashioned glass. Garnish with orange slice.

## QUEBEC

| | |
|---|---|
| 1½ ozs. Canadian whisky | ¼ oz. maraschino |
| ¼ oz. Amer Picon | liqueur |
| | ½ oz. dry vermouth |

Shake well with ice. Strain into prechilled sugar-frosted cocktail glass.

## ROB ROY

| | |
|---|---|
| 1½ to 2 ozs. Scotch | 1 dash orange bitters |
| whisky | (optional) |
| ½ oz. sweet vermouth | |

Stir well with ice. Strain into prechilled cocktail glass. The rob roy is, of course, simply a Scotch manhattan, and variations in whisky and vermouth proportions may be made to your own drinking taste. A light rather than a smoky Scotch is preferred by most people. A brandied cherry may be added for a special flourish. For a dry rob roy, use dry vermouth; add a twist of lemon if desired.

## ROB ROY, HOLIDAY STYLE

½ teaspoon Drambuie    ¼ oz. sweet vermouth
2 ozs. Scotch whisky    1 maraschino or
¼ oz. dry vermouth      brandied cherry

Pour Drambuie into a prechilled cocktail glass and swirl it around to coat bottom and sides of glass. Stir Scotch and both kinds of vermouth well with ice. Strain into glass. Add cherry.

## RUSTY NAIL

¾ oz. Scotch whisky    ¾ oz. Drambuie

Pour over rocks in prechilled old-fashioned glass. Stir.

## SAZERAC

¼ teaspoon abisante,    ¼ teaspoon bitters
   anesone or any       (Peychaud's, if
   other absinthe        possible)
   substitute    2 ozs. blended whiskey
½ teaspoon sugar      or bourbon
                Lemon peel

Swirl abisante around in prechilled old-fashioned glass until inside is completely coated. Add sugar, bitters and 1 tablespoon water. Stir until sugar is dissolved. Add a large ice cube and whiskey. Stir well. Twist lemon peel above drink and drop into glass. A New Orleans specialty and a magnificent prebrunch drink.

## SAZERAC A LA PLAYBOY

¼ teaspoon Pernod
1 small sugar cube
2 dashes Peychaud's
   bitters

1 dash Angostura
   bitters
1½ ozs. straight rye
   Lemon peel

Pour Pernod into prechilled old-fashioned glass and roll glass until inside is entirely coated. Add sugar, both kinds of bitters and enough cold water to barely cover sugar. Muddle until sugar is completely dissolved. Add whiskey and a large ice cube. Stir well. Twist lemon peel above drink and drop into glass. Created by George Crouchette, head bartender at the New Orleans Playboy Club.

## SCOTCH HOLIDAY SOUR

2 ozs. light Scotch
   whisky
1 oz. cherry liqueur
½ oz. sweet vermouth

1 oz. lemon juice
½ egg white
1 slice lemon

Shake Scotch, cherry liqueur, vermouth, lemon juice and egg white well with ice. Strain into prechilled oversize sour glass or into prechilled old-fashioned glass with a large rock. Garnish with lemon slice.

## SEABOARD

1 oz. blended whiskey
1 oz. gin
½ oz. lemon juice

1 teaspoon sugar
2 sprigs mint

Shake whiskey, gin, lemon juice and sugar well with ice. Strain over rocks in prechilled old-fashioned glass. Tear several leaves of each mint sprig before dropping into drink.

## THE SHOOT

1 oz. Scotch whisky
1 oz. dry sherry
1 teaspoon lemon juice
1 teaspoon orange juice
½ teaspoon sugar

Shake with ice. Strain into prechilled cocktail glass.

## SINGAPORE

1½ ozs. Canadian
    whisky
¼ oz. sloe gin
¼ oz. Rose's lime juice
½ oz. lemon juice
Cucumber peel

Shake whisky, sloe gin, Rose's lime juice and lemon juice well with ice. Strain over rocks in prechilled old-fashioned glass. Add cucumber peel.

## SOUTHERN GINGER

1½ ozs. 100-proof
    bourbon
1 oz. ginger ale
¼ oz. lemon juice
½ teaspoon ginger-
    flavored brandy
Lemon peel

Shake bourbon, ginger ale, lemon juice and ginger brandy well with ice. Strain into prechilled cocktail glass. Twist lemon peel above drink and drop into glass.

## STONYBROOK

1½ ozs. blended whiskey
½ oz. triple sec
¼ teaspoon orzata
½ egg white
Lemon peel
Orange peel

Shake whiskey, triple sec, orzata and egg white well with ice. Strain into prechilled cocktail glass. Twist fruit peels above drink and drop into glass.

## TROIS RIVIERES

1½ ozs. Canadian whisky ¼ oz. Cointreau
½ oz. Dubonnet Orange peel

Shake whisky, Dubonnet and Cointreau well with ice. Strain into prechilled cocktail glass. Twist orange peel above drink and drop into glass. Perfect before a midnight collation.

## TWIN HILLS

2 ozs. blended whiskey 1 teaspoon sugar
¼ oz. lemon juice ½ slice lemon
¼ oz. lime juice ½ slice lime
2 teaspoons Benedictine

Shake whiskey, lemon juice, lime juice, Benedictine and sugar well with ice. Strain into prechilled whiskey-sour glass. Garnish with lemon and lime slices.

## WARD EIGHT

2 ozs. blended U.S. 1 teaspoon sugar
   whiskey or Cana- ½ teaspoon grenadine
   dian whisky 1 slice lemon
½ oz. lemon juice

Shake whiskey, lemon juice, sugar and grenadine well with ice. Strain into tall 8-oz. glass. Add cracked ice or ice slices to fill glass. Stir. Garnish with lemon slice. A pleasant tall cocktail that survived Prohibition.

## WHISKEY SOUR

2 ozs. blended whiskey ½ slice lemon
¾ oz. lemon juice 1 maraschino cherry
1 teaspoon powdered    (optional)
   sugar

Shake whiskey, lemon juice and sugar well with ice. Strain into prechilled whiskey-sour glass. Garnish with lemon slice and cherry, if desired. For a more tart drink, reduce amount of sugar. For a more mellow whiskey sour, use ½ oz. lemon juice and ¼ oz. orange juice. Sours made with Canadian or Scotch whiskies are pleasing variants, the former having a strong appeal for the distaff side.

## WHISKEY TODDY, COLD

| | |
|---|---|
| ½ teaspoon sugar | blended whiskey |
| 2 teaspoons water | Lemon peel |
| 2 ozs. bourbon or | (optional) |

Put sugar and water into prechilled old-fashioned glass. Stir until sugar dissolves. Fill glass with ice cubes or large pieces of cracked ice. Add whiskey. Stir well. Twist lemon peel above drink and drop into glass. Must be stinging cold.

# Miscellaneous Cocktails

## ANDALUSIA

1½ ozs. very dry sherry
½ oz. cognac
½ oz. light rum

1 dash Angostura
  bitters

Stir well with ice. Strain into prechilled cocktail glass.

## BRANDIED MADEIRA

1 oz. Madeira
1 oz. brandy

½ oz. dry vermouth
  Lemon peel

Stir Madeira, brandy and vermouth well with ice. Pour over rocks in prechilled old-fashioned glass. Twist lemon peel above drink and drop into glass.

## BRANDIED PORT

1 oz. tawny port
1 oz. brandy
½ oz. lemon juice

1 teaspoon maraschino
  liqueur
1 slice orange

Shake port, brandy, lemon juice and maraschino liqueur well with ice. Strain over rocks in prechilled old-fashioned glass. Add orange slice.

## CLARET COCKTAIL

1 oz. dry red wine
1 oz. brandy
¼ oz. curaçao

¼ oz. lemon juice
½ teaspoon anisette
  Orange peel

Shake wine, brandy, curaçao, lemon juice and anisette well with ice. Strain into prechilled cocktail glass. Twist orange peel above drink and drop into glass.

## CREAMY ORANGE

1   oz. orange juice      ½   oz. cream
1   oz. cream sherry      2   teaspoons brandy

Shake well with ice. Strain into prechilled cocktail glass. A gentle introduction to a brunch omelet.

## FIORD

1   oz. brandy            ½   oz. lime juice
½   oz. aquavit           1   teaspoon grenadine
½   oz. orange juice

Shake well with ice. Strain into prechilled cocktail glass.

## FLORIDA

1¼  ozs. orange juice     ¼   oz. triple sec
½   oz. gin               1   teaspoon lemon juice
¼   oz. kirschwasser

Shake well with ice. Strain into prechilled sugar-frosted cocktail glass. A drink with less hard liquor than citrus juice, but one which always clears up the fog.

## FROZEN AQUAVIT

1½  ozs. aquavit          1   teaspoon sugar
½   oz. lime juice        1   teaspoon kirsch-
½   egg white                 wasser
½   cup crushed ice

Put all ingredients into blender. Blend at low speed 10–15 seconds. Pour into prechilled deep-saucer champagne glass.

## GENEVER COCKTAIL

1½ ozs. Dutch genever      1   teaspoon sugar
    gin                  1   dash Angostura
 ½ oz. lime juice            bitters
 ½ oz. orange juice

Shake well with ice. Strain over rocks in prechilled old-fashioned glass. Odd but very obliging.

## GRAPPA STREGA

1   oz. grappa           ¼ oz. orange juice
1   oz. Strega           Lemon peel
¼ oz. lemon juice

Shake grappa, Strega, lemon juice and orange juice well with ice. Strain into prechilled cocktail glass. Twist lemon peel above drink and drop into glass.

## KIR

3½ ozs. ice-cold dry      ½ oz. ice-cold crème
     white wine             de cassis

Pour into prechilled 7- or 8-oz. wide-bellied wineglass. Proportions may be varied, but the 7-to-1 *vin blanc*–cassis ratio above (actually a variation of the vermouth cassis) is the most commonly accepted version.

## MIDNIGHT SUN

1½ ozs. aquavit         1   teaspoon sugar
 ½ oz. unsweetened    ½ teaspoon grenadine
     grapefruit juice     ½ slice orange
 ½ oz. lemon juice

Shake aquavit, grapefruit juice, lemon juice, sugar and grenadine well with ice. Strain into prechilled whiskey-sour glass. Add orange slice.

# PERNOD DRIP

1½  ozs. Pernod                  1   cube sugar

The first requirement for this drink is an absinthe drip glass. If you don't own a drip glass, you can use a tea strainer over an old-fashioned glass as a substitute. First pour the Pernod into the glass. Place the strainer on the glass. Put the sugar over the drip section on top of the glass. Pack a mound of crushed or finely cracked ice atop the sugar. When the ice has melted, the drip is ready. Strictly for curio seekers in the spirit world.

## PISCO SOUR

1½  ozs. pisco brandy         1   tablespoon egg white
½   oz. lemon juice                 Angostura bitters
1   tablespoon sugar

Shake pisco, lemon juice, sugar and egg white well with ice. Strain into prechilled cocktail glass with sugar-frosted rim. Float a few drops bitters on top.

## ROCKY GREEN DRAGON

1   oz. gin                          ¾  oz. cognac
¾  oz. green Chartreuse

Shake extremely well with ice. Strain over rocks in prechilled old-fashioned glass. A potent dragon to be slowly sipped, not gulped.

## SUISSESSE

1½  ozs. Pernod                  ¼  oz. heavy sweet
½   oz. anisette                           cream
                                          ½  egg white

Shake well with ice. Pour into prechilled cocktail glass.

## YELLOW PLUM

1½ ozs. quetsch, mira-    1   teaspoon maraschino
    belle or slivovitz       liqueur
½ oz. lemon juice       1   teaspoon sugar
½ oz. orange juice

Shake well with ice. Strain into prechilled cocktail
glass. Tart, triumphant, titillating.

# HIGH SPIRITS

# High Spirits—Medium-Tall and King-Size Potables

If the word *highball* is heard less and less frequently these days, the drink itself is called for more and more often. Drinkers everywhere now ask for Scotch and soda, bourbon and water, applejack and ginger ale and other happy mixtures suited to their own thirst specifications. Although the highball is the easiest drink in the world to define—a small amount of something strong with a larger amount of something weak in a tall glass with ice—it's the one potable for which you seldom see a recipe. As a matter of fact, a host who, in the intimacy of his own digs, strictly follows a highball recipe is inhospitable. It's the one drink guests themselves expect to mix to their own tastes, in the same way that they salt and pepper their food. No two-finger measurements are alike and no two guests will ever say "when" at the same point on the stopwatch. Even at commuter stand-up bars, where whiskey is carefully measured in a standard jigger, the bubbly water always remains in the hands of the highballer pouring his soda, Seven-Up or tonic to his own level.

But the highball is only one of countless potables in tall glasses. A tall drink at the end of a long, tiring day can do things no short drink can ever hope to do. A wilted worthy need only look at a lofty drink clinking with ice, and miraculous changes take place within him. His collar seems to cling less tenaciously. He begins to talk in more relaxed, civilized tones. And then, as the first sip of a tall drink passes over his tongue and throat, like springwater gurgling into a hot arroyo, he feels the unparalleled pleasure of a long-delayed thrill.

One of the obvious virtues of tall mixed drinks is that they never seem to get in the way of food or vice versa. A man may hesitate to eat a trout *au bleu* while drinking a manhattan, but he won't hesitate to drink a tall spritzer of Rhine wine and soda before, during or after the trout. Although Europophilian wine pundits will be horrified at the thought, many a tall cooler at many a fine feast supplants *both* the cocktail and the wine. Ounce for ounce, a tall cooler with club soda is actually no stronger than wine. But in the final analysis, tall drinks are made not for debating but for happy guzzling.

In preparing tall drinks, whether they be 8, 12 or 20 ounces, the host should follow this modern code for presenting them:

Use a fine liquor. The flavor of a poor liquor is actually intensified in a tall drink; you have time to scrutinize it more carefully than when you down it in one gulp. This doesn't mean that you must buy a 16-year-old bonded whiskey the next time you serve a round of whiskey collinses. But you should seek one of the eminent brands of liquor that are mellow, smooth and pleasing whether taken straight or in a tall drink.

Be meticulous about the quality of the iced club soda or the ginger ale. For a small number of highballers, serve splits of soda or ginger ale. Larger bottles of carbonated waters, except for a party, just stand around going quietly flat unless you and your guests are unusually speedy drinkers.

Add bubblewater just before drinks are delivered. For optimum sparkle, pour it against the inside of the tilted glass.

Be sure the effervescent water is ice-cold so that it retains its fizz as long as possible.

Plain tap water, if used, must be clear and clean, without evidence of rust, lime, iron, chlorination or other urban evils. Use bottled springwater, if necessary, when your guests decline bubbles.

Use enough liquor in a tall drink, at least 1½ ounces in an 8-ounce glass and up to 2 ounces or more in 12- to 20-ounce glasses.

Use thin glassware with heavy bottoms to avoid the well-known sliding drink.

The gin and tonic has not only joined the tall-drink derby, but in many circles is way out in front both in summer and winter. Bitter lemon and bitter orange have joined the same fraternity. As the British Empire becomes more and more liquidated, the British-inspired bubblies seem to become more and more popular.

Among simple highballs, the whiskey highball is the best known. But there's no dogma that interdicts the use of any liquor in a highball, from aquavit to zubrovka. One of the best contemporary highballs is light, dry rum and iced club soda or iced tonic water.

So-called lowballs are actually served in glasses which hold as much as their taller cousins but which are squat in shape rather than long; old-fashioned-type glasses ranging from 7 to 11 ounces are considered lowballs.

# Bucks

Bucks are medium-long drinks—served in tall eight-ounce glasses—that always contain ginger ale and fresh lemon or lime juice. Traditionally the fruit was squeezed and dropped into the glass. You'll find you get better bucks if the lemon or lime juice is measured into the glass and the drink then garnished with a slice of fruit as its crowning touch.

## APPLE BUCK

1½  ozs. applejack
 1   teaspoon ginger-
       flavored brandy
 ½   oz. lemon juice

Iced ginger ale
 1   chunk preserved
       ginger in syrup

Shake applejack, ginger brandy and lemon juice well with ice. Strain into 8-oz. glass half-filled with ice. Add ginger ale. Stir. Add preserved ginger.

## BRANDY BUCK

1½  ozs. brandy
 1   teaspoon crème de
       menthe

½   oz. lemon juice
Iced ginger ale
Fresh grapes

Shake brandy, crème de menthe and lemon juice well with ice. Strain into 8-oz. glass half-filled with ice. Add ginger ale. Stir. Add three or four seedless grapes.

## GIN BUCK

| 1½ ozs. gin | Iced ginger ale |
| ½ oz. lemon juice | 1 slice lemon |

Shake gin and lemon juice well with ice. Strain into 8-oz. glass half-filled with ice. Add ginger ale. Stir. Add lemon slice.

## GREEK BUCK

| 1½ ozs. Metaxa brandy | 1 teaspoon ouzo |
| ½ oz. lemon juice | 1 slice lemon |
| Iced ginger ale | |

Shake Metaxa and lemon juice well with ice. Strain into 8-oz. glass half-filled with ice. Add ginger ale. Stir. Float ouzo on top of drink. Add lemon slice.

## NEW ORLEANS BUCK

| 1½ ozs. light rum | 2 dashes Peychaud's |
| ½ oz. lime juice | bitters |
| ½ oz. orange juice | Iced ginger ale |
| | 1 slice lime |

Shake rum, lime juice, orange juice and bitters well with ice. Strain into 8-oz. glass half-filled with ice. Add ginger ale. Stir. Add lime slice.

## ORANGE BUCK

| 1½ ozs. gin | Iced ginger ale |
| 1 oz. orange juice | 1 slice cocktail orange |
| ½ oz. lemon juice | in syrup |

Shake gin, orange juice and lemon juice well with ice. Strain into 8-oz. glass half-filled with ice. Add ginger ale. Stir. Add orange slice.

## PEACH BUCK

1¼ ozs. vodka
2   teaspoons peach-
       flavored brandy
½ oz. lemon juice

Iced ginger ale
1   slice lemon
1   slice fresh or
       brandied peach

Shake vodka, peach-flavored brandy and lemon juice
well with ice. Strain into 8-oz. glass half-filled with
ice. Add ginger ale. Stir. Garnish with lemon and
peach slices.

## RUM BUCK

1½ ozs. light rum
½ oz. lime juice
   Iced ginger ale

1   slice lime
   Toasted slivered
      almonds

Shake rum and lime juice well with ice. Strain into
8-oz. glass half-filled with ice. Add ginger ale. Stir. Add
lime slice and about a teaspoon of almonds.

# Cobblers

Like a fix, see page 185, a cobbler is concocted in the glass without club soda, quinine water or any other sparkling dilutants. Though the recipes that follow are designed to fill a 12-ounce glass, they can be extended or abbreviated to fit your own glassware.

## BRANDY COBBLER

| | |
|---|---|
| 1½ ozs. brandy | 1 teaspoon kirsch-wasser |
| ½ oz. curaçao | |
| ½ oz. lemon juice | 1 cocktail pineapple stick |
| 1 teaspoon sugar | |

Fill a 12-oz. glass with finely cracked ice. Add brandy, curaçao, lemon juice, sugar and kirschwasser. Stir well until sugar is dissolved. Add more ice to fill glass to rim. Stir. Garnish with pineapple stick.

## CHERRY COBBLER

| | |
|---|---|
| 1½ ozs. gin | 1 teaspoon sugar |
| ½ oz. Cherry Heering or Cherry Karise | ½ oz. lemon juice |
| | 1 slice lemon |
| ½ oz. crème de cassis | 1 maraschino cherry |

Fill a 12-oz. glass with finely cracked ice. Add gin, Cherry Heering, crème de cassis, sugar and lemon juice. Stir well until sugar dissolves. Add more ice to fill glass to rim. Stir. Add lemon slice and cherry.

## CLARET COBBLER

| | |
|---|---|
| 4 ozs. dry red wine | ½ oz. maraschino liqueur |
| ½ oz. lemon juice | |
| ½ oz. orange juice | ½ slice orange |
| | ½ slice lime |

Fill a 12-oz. glass with finely cracked ice. Add wine, lemon juice, orange juice and maraschino liqueur. Stir well. Add more ice to fill glass to rim. Stir. Garnish with orange and lime slices.

## PORT COBBLER

| | |
|---|---|
| 4   ozs. tawny port | Lemon peel |
| ¾   oz. brandy | Orange peel |
| ½   teaspoon sugar | 2   large mint leaves |

Fill a 12-oz. glass with finely cracked ice. Add port, brandy and sugar. Stir well. Add more ice to fill glass to rim. Stir. Twist lemon peel and orange peel above drink and drop into glass. Tear mint leaves partially and drop into glass.

## SHERRY COBBLER

| | |
|---|---|
| 2½  ozs. sherry | ½   teaspoon sugar |
| 1   oz. brandy | 1   slice cocktail orange |
| ½   oz. orange juice |      in syrup |

Fill a 12-oz. glass with finely cracked ice. Add sherry, brandy, orange juice and sugar. Stir well until sugar dissolves. Add more ice to fill glass to rim. Stir. Garnish with orange slice.

## WHISKEY COBBLER

| | |
|---|---|
| 2½  ozs. blended whiskey | ½   slice orange |
| ¾   oz. lemon juice | 1   slice fresh or |
| ½   oz. grapefruit juice |      brandied peach |
| 1½  teaspoons orgeat or | |
|      orzata | |

Fill a 12-oz. glass with finely cracked ice. Add whiskey, lemon juice, grapefruit juice and orgeat. Stir well. Add more ice to fill glass to rim. Stir. Garnish with orange and peach slices.

# Collinses

Among the oldest and best-known tall summer drinks, collinses always start with liquor, lemon juice and soda and bear a striking resemblance to fizzes (page 189). A tom collins and a gin fizz are for all practical purposes the same drink. Some bartenders dress up the collins with orange slices, cherries and other bits of fruit, although this practice is frowned upon by veteran benders at the bar.

## APPLEJACK COLLINS

| | |
|---|---|
| 2   ozs. applejack | 2   dashes orange |
| 1   teaspoon sugar | bitters |
| 1   oz. lemon juice | Iced club soda |
| | 1   slice lemon |

Shake applejack, sugar, lemon juice and bitters well with ice. Strain into tall 14-oz. glass half-filled with ice. Add soda. Stir. Add lemon slice.

## B & B COLLINS

| | |
|---|---|
| 2   ozs. cognac | Iced club soda |
| ½   oz. lemon juice | ½   oz. Benedictine |
| 1   teaspoon sugar | 1   slice lemon |

Shake cognac, lemon juice and sugar well with ice. Strain into tall 14-oz. glass half-filled with ice. Add soda. Stir. Float Benedictine on drink. Add lemon slice.

## BOURBON COLLINS

2 ozs. 100-proof
    bourbon
2 dashes Peychaud's
    bitters

½ oz. lemon juice
1 teaspoon sugar
  Iced club soda
1 slice lemon

Shake bourbon, bitters, lemon juice and sugar well with ice. Strain into tall 14-oz. glass half-filled with ice. Add soda. Stir. Add lemon slice.

## BRANDIED BANANA COLLINS

1½ ozs. brandy
1 oz. banana liqueur
½ oz. lemon juice

  Iced club soda
1 slice lemon
1 slice banana

Shake brandy, banana liqueur and lemon juice well with ice. Strain into tall 14-oz. glass half-filled with ice. Add soda. Stir. Add lemon and banana slices.

## COEXISTENCE COLLINS

2 ozs. vodka
½ oz. lemon juice
1 teaspoon sugar
1 teaspoon kümmel
  Iced club soda

Cucumber peel, 2
  inches long, ½
  inch wide
Lemon peel

Shake vodka, lemon juice, sugar and kümmel well with ice. Strain into tall 14-oz. glass half-filled with ice. Add soda. Stir. Add cucumber peel. Twist lemon peel above drink and drop into glass.

## JOHN COLLINS

Same drink as tom collins except made with Dutch genever gin.

## MINT COLLINS

| | |
|---|---|
| 2   ozs. gin | ½  cup crushed ice |
| 4   large mint leaves | Iced club soda |
| ½  oz. lemon juice | 1   slice lemon |
| 1   teaspoon sugar | |

Put gin, mint leaves, lemon juice, sugar and crushed ice into blender. Blend at high speed 15 seconds or until mint leaves are finely chopped. Pour into tall 14-oz. glass. Add soda to fill glass. Stir. Add lemon slice.

## TOM COLLINS

| | |
|---|---|
| 2   to 2½ ozs. gin | 1   slice orange |
| 1   to 2 teaspoons sugar | (optional) |
| ½  to 1 oz. lemon juice | 1   maraschino cherry |
| Iced club soda | (optional) |
| 1   slice lemon | |
| (optional) | |

Shake gin, sugar and lemon juice well with ice. Strain into tall 14-oz. glass half-filled with ice. Add soda. Stir. Add lemon slice and/or orange slice and/or cherry.

# Coolers—Miscellaneous Tall Drinks

For every taste, for every mood, for every summer day, the following potpourri of coolers and icy tall drinks will be as welcome as the trade winds to becalmed vessels on a sweltering sea.

## AMER PICON COOLER

1½ ozs. Amer Picon
1 oz. gin
½ oz. cherry liqueur
½ oz. lemon juice
1 teaspoon sugar
Iced club soda

Shake Amer Picon, gin, cherry liqueur, lemon juice and sugar well with ice. Strain into tall 14-oz. glass half-filled with ice. Add soda. Stir.

## APPLE BRANDY COOLER

2 ozs. brandy
1 oz. light rum
3 ozs. apple juice
½ oz. lime juice
1 teaspoon dark
    Jamaican rum
1 slice lime

Shake brandy, light rum, apple juice and lime juice well with ice. Strain into tall 14-oz. glass. Add ice to fill glass. Stir. Float dark rum on drink. Add lime slice.

## APPLE KNOCKER

2½ ozs. applejack
½ oz. sweet vermouth
3 ozs. orange juice
½ oz. lemon juice
1½ teaspoons sugar
½ cup crushed ice

Put all ingredients into blender. Blend at high speed 15–20 seconds. Pour into tall 14-oz. glass. Let drink settle a moment. Add ice to fill glass. Stir.

## BEER BUSTER

1½ ozs. ice-cold 100-
    proof vodka
    Ice-cold beer or ale

2  dashes Tabasco
    sauce

Pour vodka, beer and Tabasco sauce into prechilled
tall 14-oz. glass or beer mug. Stir lightly. A drink for
those who like to key up with beer rather than with
cocktails before dinner, for football fans hoarse from
cheering, for men who like a long, cold drink with their
bubbling-hot Welsh rabbit and for cheese connoisseurs
with a thirst.

## BITTER BANANA COOLER

1½ ozs. light rum
¼ cup sliced banana
¼ cup pineapple juice
½ oz. lime juice

2  dashes Peychaud's
    bitters
½ cup crushed ice
    Iced bitter-lemon
    soda

Put rum, sliced banana, pineapple juice, lime juice,
bitters and crushed ice into blender. Blend 10–15
seconds at high speed. Pour into tall 14-oz. glass. Let
foamy cap of drink settle somewhat. Add two ice cubes.
Fill glass with bitter-lemon soda.

## BITTER BOURBON LEMONADE

2  ozs. bourbon
1  oz. lemon juice
½ oz. lime juice
1  teaspoon grenadine

1  teaspoon sugar
    Iced bitter-lemon
    soda
1  slice lemon

Shake bourbon, lemon juice, lime juice, grenadine and
sugar well with ice. Strain into tall 14-oz. glass. Add
two ice cubes. Fill glass with bitter-lemon soda. Garnish
with lemon slice. A bittersweet pleasure.

## BITTER BRANDY AND SHERRY

| | |
|---|---|
| 1   oz. brandy | 1   teaspoon lemon juice |
| 1   oz. oloroso (cream) | Iced bitter-lemon |
|      sherry |      soda |
| ½  oz. cherry liqueur | 1   slice lemon |

Shake brandy, sherry, cherry liqueur and lemon juice well with ice. Strain into tall 14-oz. glass with two large ice cubes. Add soda. Stir. Add lemon slice.

## BITTER-LEMON COOLER

| | |
|---|---|
| 1½  ozs. dry vermouth | 1   teaspoon lemon |
| 1    oz. gin |      juice |
| 1    teaspoon raspberry | Iced bitter-lemon |
|       syrup |      soda |
| | Lemon peel |

Shake vermouth, gin, raspberry syrup and lemon juice well with ice. Strain into tall 14-oz. glass containing two large ice cubes. Add bitter-lemon soda. Stir. Twist lemon peel above drink and drop into glass.

## BITTER-ORANGE COOLER

| | |
|---|---|
| 2½  ozs. orange juice | Iced bitter-orange |
| 3    ozs. sweet vermouth |      soda |
| ½   oz. lemon juice | 1   slice orange |
| ½   oz. cherry liqueur | |

Shake orange juice, vermouth, lemon juice and cherry liqueur well with ice. Pour into tall 14-oz. glass with two large ice cubes. Add soda. Stir. Garnish with orange slice.

## BLENDED COMFORT

| | | | |
|---|---|---|---|
| 2 | ozs. blended whiskey | 1 | oz. orange juice |
| ½ | oz. Southern Comfort | ½ | cup crushed ice |
| ¼ | cup thawed frozen peaches | 1 | slice lemon |
| ½ | oz. dry vermouth | 1 | slice cocktail orange in syrup |
| 1½ | ozs. lemon juice | | |

Put whiskey, Southern Comfort, peaches, vermouth, lemon juice, orange juice and crushed ice into blender. Blend 10–15 seconds. Pour into tall 14-oz. glass. Add ice to fill glass. Garnish with lemon and orange slices.

## BRANDIED PEACH SLING

| | | | |
|---|---|---|---|
| 1¾ | ozs. brandy | | Iced club soda |
| ½ | oz. peach-flavored brandy | 1 | slice brandied or thawed frozen peach |
| ¾ | oz. lemon juice | | |
| 1 | teaspoon sugar | | Lemon peel |

Shake brandy, peach-flavored brandy, lemon juice and sugar well with ice. Strain into tall 14-oz. glass half-filled with ice. Add soda. Stir. Add peach slice. Twist lemon peel above drink and drop into glass.

## BRIGHTON PUNCH

| | | | |
|---|---|---|---|
| 1 | oz. bourbon | ½ | oz. lemon juice |
| 1 | oz. cognac | 1 | oz. iced club soda |
| ¾ | oz. Benedictine | ½ | slice orange |
| 1 | oz. orange juice | 1 | slice lemon |

Shake bourbon, cognac, Benedictine, orange juice and lemon juice well with ice. Strain into tall 14-oz. glass. Add soda and enough ice to fill glass. Stir. Garnish with orange and lemon slices.

## BUNNY MOTHER

1¼  ozs. vodka
1   oz. orange juice
1   oz. lemon juice
1   teaspoon sugar

¼   oz. grenadine
¼   oz. Cointreau
½   slice orange
1   maraschino cherry

Shake vodka, orange juice, lemon juice, sugar and grenadine well with ice. Strain into prechilled 12-oz. mug. Add coarsely cracked ice to fill mug to ½ inch from top. Float Cointreau on top. Garnish with orange slice and cherry, as served at the San Francisco Playboy Club.

## BYRRH CASSIS COOLER

2   ozs. Byrrh
½   oz. crème de cassis

Iced club soda
1   slice lemon

Put ice cubes up to the rim in a tall 14-oz. glass. Add Byrrh and crème de cassis. Add soda. Stir. Garnish with lemon slice. Quickens the appetite even though slightly sweet. Nice to hold in your hands when the *blanquette de veau* is simmering in the kitchen.

## CALYPSO COOLER

2½  ozs. light rum
1   oz. frozen concen-
       trated pineapple
       juice, thawed but
       not diluted
½   oz. lime juice

1   teaspoon sugar
    Iced club soda
1   thin slice fresh
       pineapple
1   slice lime

Shake rum, pineapple juice, lime juice and sugar well with ice. Strain into tall 14-oz. glass. Add a splash of soda and ice to fill glass. Garnish with pineapple and lime slices.

## CARTHUSIAN COOLER

| | |
|---|---|
| 1 oz. yellow Chartreuse | Iced club soda |
| 1 oz. bourbon | |

Put three large ice cubes into a tall 14-oz. glass. Add Chartreuse and bourbon. Fill glass with soda. Stir.

## CHABLIS COOLER

| | |
|---|---|
| ½ oz. grenadine | 1 oz. vodka |
| ½ oz. lemon juice | Iced Chablis |
| ¼ teaspoon vanilla extract | |

Sugar-frost a tall 14-oz. glass. Pour grenadine, lemon juice, vanilla extract and vodka into glass. Stir well. Add three large ice cubes. Fill glass to rim with Chablis. Stir.

## CHARTREUSE COOLER

| | |
|---|---|
| 1 oz. yellow Chartreuse | Iced bitter-lemon soda |
| 3 ozs. orange juice | 1 slice orange |
| 1 oz. lemon juice | |

Shake Chartreuse, orange juice and lemon juice well with ice. Strain into tall 14-oz. glass half-filled with ice. Fill glass with bitter-lemon soda. Add orange slice.

## CLARET COOLER

| | |
|---|---|
| 4 ozs. chilled dry red wine | 3 ozs. iced club soda |
| ½ oz. brandy | Orange rind, 3 inches long, ½ inch wide |
| 1 oz. orange juice | 1 slice lemon |
| ½ oz. lemon juice | |

Pour wine, brandy, orange juice, lemon juice and soda into tall 14-oz. glass. Add ice cubes or cracked ice to fill glass. Stir. Place orange rind in drink. Float lemon slice on top.

## CLARET RUM COOLER

| | |
|---|---|
| 3 ozs. chilled dry red wine | 3 ozs. iced club soda |
| 1 oz. light rum | 1 slice orange |
| ½ oz. kirschwasser | 1 large fresh strawberry |
| ½ oz. Falernum | |

Pour wine, rum, kirschwasser, Falernum and soda into tall 14-oz. glass. Add ice cubes or cracked ice to fill glass. Stir. Garnish with orange slice and strawberry.

## COCONUT COOLER IN SHELL

| | |
|---|---|
| 1 coconut | 1½ ozs. light rum |
| ½ cup crushed ice | 1 oz. cream |
| 1 oz. canned cream of coconut | |

Remove end of coconut opposite coconut eyes. The best procedure is to hold the base of the coconut firmly in the left hand. With a very heavy French knife or cleaver, chop top off by striking coconut glancing blows diagonally. Several whacks may be necessary. Avoid spilling coconut juice if possible. Pour out coconut juice and save it. Into blender, pour ¼ cup coconut juice, ice, cream of coconut, rum and cream. Blend at high speed 10 seconds. Pour into coconut shell. Place coconut shell in large dish surrounded with finely crushed ice. There will usually be enough juice from one coconut for three or four drinks. Reserve drinks may be made up beforehand, poured into a pitcher and stored in the refrigerator. Coconut shells may then be refilled when necessary. Byron once said nothing calmed the spirit as much as rum and true religion. The balmy beneficence of the preceding recipe will bear out that astute poet to the fullest.

## COFFEE COOLER

| | |
|---|---|
| 4 ozs. cold coffee | 1 teaspoon sugar |
| 1½ ozs. vodka | 1 small dip coffee ice |
| 1 oz. cream | cream |
| 1 oz. coffee liqueur | |

Shake coffee, vodka, cream, coffee liqueur and sugar well with ice. Strain into tall 14-oz. glass. Add ice cream. A sweet cooler that serves as both iced coffee and dessert in one glass.

## COFFEE EGGNOG

| | |
|---|---|
| 1½ ozs. Canadian whisky | 1 teaspoon sugar |
| 1 oz. coffee liqueur | ½ teaspoon instant coffee |
| 1 small egg | Ground coriander seed |
| 4 ozs. milk | |
| ½ oz. cream | |

Shake whisky, coffee liqueur, egg, milk, cream, sugar and instant coffee with ice extremely well—about twice the usual mixing time. Strain into tall 14-oz. glass. Sprinkle with coriander.

## COLD IRISH

1½  ozs. Irish whiskey
2   teaspoons Irish Mist
       liqueur
    Iced coffee soda

Sweetened whipped
    cream
Crème de cacao

Pour whiskey and Irish Mist into tall 14-oz. glass. Add
one large ice cube. Fill glass to within 1 inch of top
with soda. Stir. Flavor whipped cream with crème de
cacao, using ½ oz. crème de cacao for each ½ cup
heavy cream used for whipping. Add a large dollop of
whipped-cream topping to drink.

## COOL COLONEL

1½  ozs. bourbon
1   oz. Southern
       Comfort
3   ozs. chilled strong
       black tea

2   teaspoons lemon juice
2   teaspoons sugar
    Iced club soda

Pour bourbon, Southern Comfort, tea, lemon juice and
sugar into tall 14-oz. glass. Stir until sugar dissolves.
Add two large ice cubes and a splash of soda. Stir.
Breathe deeply. Tilt head. Bend elbow.

## CORDIAL MEDOC CUP

1   oz. Cordial Médoc
½  oz. cognac
1   oz. lemon juice

½  teaspoon sugar
    Iced brut champagne
1   slice orange

Shake Cordial Médoc, cognac, lemon juice and sugar
well with ice. Strain into 10-oz. glass with two large
ice cubes. Fill glass with champagne. Stir very slightly.
Add orange slice. A tall drink for toasting.

## CREAMY SCREWDRIVER

| | |
|---|---|
| 2  ozs. vodka | 6  ozs. orange juice |
| 1  small egg yolk or ½ large yolk, slightly beaten | ¾ cup finely cracked ice |
| | 1  teaspoon sugar |

Put all ingredients into well of blender. Blend about 20 seconds. Pour over two or three ice cubes in tall 14-oz. glass. Add more ice cubes if necessary to fill glass. A prebrunch potation.

## CUBA LIBRE

| | |
|---|---|
| 2  ozs. golden  rum | Iced cola drink |
| ½ lime | |

Half fill a tall 14-oz. glass with coarsely chopped ice or ice cubes. Add rum. Squeeze lime above drink and drop into glass. Fill with cola. Stir well. Heavier rums such as Jamaican or Martinique may be used in place of golden rum or may be mixed half-and-half with it. A teaspoon of 151-proof rum may be floated on top of drink for a rummy bite.

## CUCUMBER CHAMPAGNE

| | |
|---|---|
| Cucumber peel | 8  ozs. iced brut champagne |
| 1  oz. Benedictine | |
| ½ oz. lemon juice | |

Prechill a 10-oz. Pilsner glass. Wash cucumber, rubbing with a vegetable brush or towel if necessary to remove any waxy coating. Cut a long strip of peel, about ½ inch wide, the entire length of the cucumber. Place in glass. Pour Benedictine and lemon juice into glass. Slowly add champagne. Stir very slightly. Let drink set a few minutes for flavors to ripen.

## CURAÇAO COOLER

| | |
|---|---|
| 1 oz. blue curaçao | Iced orange juice |
| 1 oz. vodka | Lemon peel |
| ½ oz. lime juice | Lime peel |
| ½ oz. lemon juice | Orange peel |

Shake curaçao, vodka, lime juice and lemon juice well with ice. Strain into tall 14-oz. glass. Add two large ice cubes. Fill glass with orange juice. Stir well. Twist each of the peels above the drink and drop into glass.

## DOUBLE DERBY

| | |
|---|---|
| 2½ ozs. bourbon | 1 oz. orange juice |
| 2 ozs. cold strong black tea | ½ oz. lemon juice |
| 2 ozs. claret | 1 slice cocktail orange in syrup |
| 1 oz. red-currant syrup | |

Pour bourbon, tea, claret, red-currant syrup, orange juice and lemon juice into double old-fashioned glass. Add ice cubes to fill to brim. Stir well. Add orange slice. If red-currant syrup is not available, red-currant jelly to which a teaspoon of hot water has been added may be heated over a low flame and stirred constantly until jelly is liquid.

## DRY-MANHATTAN COOLER

| | |
|---|---|
| 2 ozs. blended whiskey | ½ oz. orgeat or orzata |
| 1 oz. dry vermouth | Iced club soda |
| 2 ozs. orange juice | 1 maraschino cherry |
| ½ oz. lemon juice | |

Shake whiskey, vermouth, orange juice, lemon juice and orgeat well with ice. Strain into tall 14-oz. glass. Add ice to fill glass. Stir. Add cherry.

## ENGLISH MULE

| | |
|---|---|
| 3 ozs. ice-cold green-ginger wine | Iced club soda |
| 1½ ozs. gin | 1 piece preserved ginger in syrup |
| 2½ ozs. ice-cold orange juice | |

Put three ice cubes into tall 14-oz. glass. Pour wine, gin and orange juice into glass. Stir well. Fill glass with soda. Stir slightly. Fasten preserved ginger, well drained, onto cocktail spear. Fit spear into straw in glass.

## FRENCH FOAM

| | |
|---|---|
| 1 teaspoon sugar | 1 teaspoon kirschwasser |
| 1 dash Angostura bitters | 1 split ice-cold brut champagne |
| 1 teaspoon brandy | Lemon sherbet |

Put sugar, bitters, brandy and kirschwasser into 10-oz. Pilsner glass. Stir with a tall stirring rod until sugar dissolves. Fill glass three-quarters full with champagne. Float a small scoop of sherbet on top. The scoop should contain no more than 2 liquid ounces (a parfait scoop). If such a scoop is not available, use a tablespoon to add the small amount of sherbet.

## FRENCH 75

| | |
|---|---|
| 1½ ozs. cognac | 1 teaspoon sugar |
| 1 oz. lemon juice | Iced brut champagne |

Shake cognac, lemon juice and sugar well with cracked ice. Strain into 10-oz. glass with two large ice cubes. Fill to rim with champagne. Stir very slightly. Gin is sometimes substituted for cognac, making a champagne collins out of this tall classic.

# GEORGIA RUM COOLER

2½ ozs. light rum
1 teaspoon salted
   peanuts
½ oz. lemon juice
1 teaspoon grenadine

1 teaspoon Falernum
½ cup crushed ice
Iced club soda
Ground cinnamon

Put rum, peanuts, lemon juice, grenadine, Falernum
and crushed ice into blender. Blend at high speed 30
seconds. Pour into tall 14-oz. glass. Let froth on drink
settle. Add two ice cubes and a splash of soda. Stir.
Sprinkle lightly with cinnamon. Pass a platter of cold
country ham sliced paper-thin.

# GIN SWIZZLE

2 ozs. gin
½ teaspoon Angostura
   bitters

½ oz. lime juice
1 teaspoon sugar
Iced club soda

Shake gin, bitters, lime juice and sugar well with ice.
Strain into tall 14-oz. glass half-filled with ice. Add
soda. Stir. A patriarchal drink invented when swizzle
sticks were smart. Toothsome tipple now best handled
in cocktail shaker and tall glass.

# GRANADA

1 oz. very dry (fino)
   sherry
1 oz. brandy

½ oz. curaçao
Iced tonic water
1 slice orange

Shake sherry, brandy and curaçao well with ice. Pour
into tall 14-oz. glass. Add two large ice cubes. Add
tonic water. Stir. Add orange slice.

## GRAPEFRUIT COOLER

2 ozs. blended whiskey   1 teaspoon lemon juice
4 ozs. unsweetened   ½ slice orange
   grapefruit juice   ½ slice lemon
½ oz. red-currant syrup

Shake whiskey, grapefruit juice, red-currant syrup and
lemon juice well with ice. Strain into tall 14-oz. glass.
Add ice to fill glass. Stir. Garnish with orange and
lemon slices.

## GRAPEFRUIT NOG

½ cup unsweetened   1½ ozs. brandy
   grapefruit juice   1 small egg
1 oz. lemon juice   ½ cup crushed ice
1 tablespoon honey

Put all ingredients into blender. Blend 20 seconds. Pour
into double old-fashioned glass or tall 14-oz. glass.
Add ice cubes to fill glass.

## GUAVA COOLER

1½ ozs. rum   ½ oz. lemon juice
1½ ozs. guava nectar   ½ oz. pineapple juice
½ teaspoon sugar   Iced club soda
½ oz. maraschino   1 canned guava shell
   liqueur   ½ slice lemon

Shake rum, guava nectar, sugar, maraschino liqueur,
lemon juice and pineapple juice well with ice. Strain
into tall 14-oz. glass half-filled with ice. Add soda.
Stir. Garnish with guava shell and lemon slice. Wonderful cooler before or with a jambalaya feast.

## HONEYDEW COOLER

⅓ cup diced ripe            ¾ oz. lemon juice
    honeydew melon     ½ teaspoon sugar
1½ ozs. gin                 ½ cup crushed ice
¼ teaspoon Pernod              Iced club soda
1 tablespoon cream

Put honeydew, gin, Pernod, cream, lemon juice, sugar
and crushed ice into blender. Blend at low speed
15–20 seconds. Pour into tall 14-oz. glass. When foam
settles, add a splash of soda and ice to fill glass to rim,
if necessary.

## HORSE'S NECK WITH GIN

  Peel of whole lemon       ½ oz. lemon juice
2 ozs. gin                      Iced ginger ale

To peel lemon, start at stem end, using a sharp paring
knife, and cut peel about ½ inch wide in a continuous
strip until lemon is completely peeled. Place peel in a
14-oz. highball glass so that the top of peel overlaps
rim of glass, with the rest spiraling down into glass.
Fill glass with coarsely cracked ice. Pour gin and
lemon juice into glass. Fill with ginger ale. Stir.

## ICED RUM COFFEE

1½ ozs. light rum              Sugar
1 teaspoon dark          2 tablespoons sweet-
   Jamaican rum            ened whipped
6 ozs. iced double-             cream
   strength coffee

Pour rums and coffee into tall 14-oz. glass. Add ice to
fill glass. Add sugar to taste. Top with whipped cream.

## ICED RUM TEA

| | |
|---|---|
| 1½ ozs. light rum | 1 teaspoon Falernum |
| ½ oz. 151-proof rum | 1 teaspoon lemon juice |
| 6 ozs. iced strong | 1 slice lemon |
| black tea | 2 large mint leaves |
| 1 teaspoon sugar | |

Pour rums, tea, sugar, Falernum and lemon juice into tall 14-oz. glass. Add ice to fill glass. Stir. Garnish with lemon slice and mint leaves partially torn. To prevent tea clouding, let it cool to room temperature before combining with ice.

## INDEPENDENCE SWIZZLE

| | |
|---|---|
| 2 ozs. dark Trinidad | 1 teaspoon honey |
| rum | 1 teaspoon sugar |
| 3 dashes Angostura | ½ oz. lime juice |
| bitters | 1 slice lime |

In tall 14-oz. glass, stir rum, bitters, honey, sugar and lime juice until honey is blended with other ingredients. Add finely cracked ice to fill glass. Twirl with a swizzle stick if you have one, or stir and churn with a barspoon or iced-tea spoon. As drink is stirred, ice will melt. Add more ice as necessary to fill glass to rim, swizzling or stirring until ice and liquids reach top of glass. Garnish with lime slice. A drink used to celebrate the independence of Trinidad and Tobago.

## JAMAICA ELEGANCE

| | |
|---|---|
| 1½ ozs. golden | 1 oz. lime juice |
| Jamaican rum | 1 teaspoon simple |
| ½ oz. brandy | syrup |
| ½ oz. pineapple juice | 1 slice lime |

Shake rum, brandy, pineapple juice, lime juice and syrup well with ice. Strain into prechilled tall 14-oz.

glass. Add ice to fill glass. Add lime slice. Created by
C. Scott, of the Jamaica Playboy Club-Hotel.

## JAMAICA GINGER

1½ ozs. light rum
½ oz. dark Jamaican
   rum
½ oz. 151-proof rum
½ oz. Falernum
½ oz. lime juice

Iced ginger beer
½ slice pineapple in
   crème de menthe
1 cube preserved
   ginger in syrup

Shake the three kinds of rum, Falernum and lime juice
well with ice. Strain into tall 14-oz. glass half-filled with
ice. Fill glass with ginger beer. Stir. Garnish with
pineapple and ginger.

## JOCOSE JULEP

2½ ozs. bourbon
½ oz. green crème de
   menthe
6 mint leaves

1 teaspoon sugar
1 oz. lime juice
   Iced club soda
3 tall mint sprigs

Put into blender, without ice, bourbon, crème de
menthe, 6 mint leaves, sugar and lime juice. Blend
10–15 seconds or until mint is very finely chopped.
Pour into tall 14-oz. glass half-filled with ice. Add
soda. Stir. Insert mint sprigs. Serve to nearest belle.

## KERRY COOLER

2 ozs. Irish whiskey
1½ ozs. Madeira or
   sherry
1 oz. orgeat

1 oz. lemon juice
   Iced club soda
1 slice lemon

Into tall 14-oz. glass, pour whiskey, Madeira, orgeat
and lemon juice. Stir well. Add three large ice cubes.
Fill glass with soda. Stir. Float lemon slice on top.

## KIRSCH CUBA LIBRE

1½ ozs. kirschwasser          Iced cola drink
½ lime

Put three large ice cubes into a tall 14-oz. glass. Add
kirschwasser. Squeeze lime above drink and drop into
glass. Fill with cola. Stir.

## LEMON RUM COOLER

2  ozs. light rum            ½ oz. Falernum
1  teaspoon 151-proof        Iced bitter-lemon
   rum                          soda
2  ozs. pineapple juice      1  slice lemon
½ oz. lemon juice

Shake both kinds of rum, pineapple juice, lemon juice
and Falernum well with ice. Strain into tall 14-oz. glass.
Add two ice cubes. Fill glass with bitter-lemon soda.
Add lemon slice.

## MANGO COOLER

3  ozs. ice-cold mango       1½ ozs. ice-cold orange
   nectar                       juice
1½ ozs. vodka                ½ oz. Cointreau
½ oz. ice-cold lemon         1  slice orange
   juice                     1  slice mango, if in
                                season

Into tall 14-oz. glass, pour mango nectar, vodka, lemon
juice, orange juice and Cointreau. Add ice to fill glass.
Garnish with orange and mango slices. A fruity libation
to serve before an oriental or Polynesian menu.

# MINT JULEP

| 12 | mint leaves on stem | 2½ | ozs. 86- or 100-proof |
|----|---------------------|----|-----------------------|
| 1  | teaspoon sugar      |    | bourbon               |
| 2  | teaspoons water     | 6  | mint leaves on stem   |

Tear the 12 mint leaves partially while leaving them on stem. Place in tall 12-oz. glass or silver julep mug with sugar and water. Muddle or stir until sugar is completely dissolved. Fill glass with finely cracked ice. Add bourbon. Stir. Ice will dissolve partially. Add more ice to fill glass to rim, again stirring. Tear the 6 mint leaves partially to release aroma and insert into ice with leaves on top. Serve with or without straw.

## MINT JULEP, DRY, PARTY STYLE
(Serves 8)

| 1 | quart bourbon | 1 | pint finely chopped |
|---|---------------|---|---------------------|
| 8 | sprigs mint   |   | mint leaves         |

Steep mint leaves in bourbon for 1 hour at room temperature. Fill eight tall 14-oz. glasses with finely cracked ice. Strain bourbon and pour into glasses, allowing 4 ozs. minted bourbon per glass. Stir. Add more ice to fill glass to rim. Tear a few leaves of each of the mint sprigs and fit a sprig into each glass. If your party is late getting started, store prepared juleps in freezer. A few sips of this unsweetened julep should turn the longest of hot summer days into the coolest.

## MOBILE MULE

| 2 | ozs. light rum | Iced ginger beer |
|---|----------------|------------------|
| ½ | lime           |                  |

Pour rum into tall 12- or 14-oz. glass or copper mug with ice cubes or cracked ice. Squeeze lime above drink and drop into glass. Fill with ginger beer. Stir. A switch on the vodka-inspired moscow mule.

## MOSCOW MULE

1½ to 2 ozs. vodka          Iced ginger beer
½ lime

Pour vodka into tall 12- or 14-oz. glass or copper mug
with ice cubes or cracked ice. Squeeze lime above
drink and drop into glass. Fill with ginger beer. Stir.

## NECTARINE COOLER

2 ozs. vodka                1 teaspoon sugar
3 ozs. iced orange          ⅓ cup crushed ice
   juice                     Iced club soda
¼ cup cold sliced ripe      1 slice fresh nectarine
   nectarine                1 slice lemon

Put vodka, orange juice, nectarine, sugar and crushed
ice into blender. Blend at low speed 15–20 seconds.
Pour into tall 14-oz. glass. Add a splash of soda and
ice to fill glass. Stir. Garnish with nectarine and lemon
slices.

## ORANGE COOLER IN SHELL

1 extra-large California    ½ oz. lime juice
   orange                   1 teaspoon sugar
1 oz. 151-proof rum         1 slice cocktail orange
½ oz. curaçao                 in syrup

Cut a cap off top of orange about ½ inch from top.
With a sharp grapefruit knife, gouge out the meat,
leaving orange shell intact. Squeeze enough juice from
meat to make 1½ ozs. Shake orange juice, rum, curaçao, lime juice and sugar well with ice. Strain into
orange shell. Place orange shell in a bowl or soup dish
about 7 inches in diameter. Pack finely crushed ice
around orange. Fasten orange slice onto cocktail
spear and place across orange cup. Serve with a short
colored straw.

## ORANGE OASIS

| | |
|---|---|
| 4 ozs. ice-cold fresh orange juice | ½ oz. cherry liqueur  Iced ginger ale |
| 1½ ozs. gin | 1 slice orange |

Pour orange juice, gin and cherry liqueur into tall 14-oz. glass. Add ice cubes or ice slices to rim of glass. Add ginger ale. Stir. Garnish with orange slice.

## PANAMA COOLER

| | |
|---|---|
| 2 ozs. iced Rhine wine | ½ oz. maraschino liqueur |
| 2 ozs. iced very dry sherry | 1 dash Angostura bitters |
| 1 oz. orange juice | 1 oz. iced club soda |
| 1 teaspoon lime juice | 1 slice lemon |

Shake Rhine wine, sherry, orange juice, lime juice, maraschino liqueur and bitters well with ice. Strain into tall 14-oz. glass. Add soda. Fill glass with ice. Stir. Add lemon slice.

## PASSION-FRUIT COOLER

| | |
|---|---|
| 4 ozs. passion-fruit nectar (not syrup) | ½ oz. lemon juice |
| 2½ ozs. light rum | 1 oz. orange juice |
| 1 oz. gin | 2 sprigs mint |

Shake passion-fruit nectar, rum, gin, lemon juice and orange juice well with ice. Strain into tall 14-oz. glass. Add enough coarsely cracked ice or ice cubes to fill glass. Decorate with mint after partially tearing several leaves to release fragrance.

## PIMM'S CUP

1½ ozs. Pimm's No. 1          1 slice lemon
    Cup                         Cucumber peel
Iced Seven-Up or
    lemon soda

Pour Pimm's Cup into 8- or 10-oz. glass or Pimm's
glass tankard with ice. Fill with Seven-Up. Add lemon
slice and cucumber peel. Stir. The old English gin sling
is bottled as Pimm's No. 1 Cup, made with a gin base
and fruit flavors.

## PINEAPPLE MINT COOLER

2  ozs. gin                     Iced club soda
½  oz. white crème de        1 cocktail pineapple
    menthe                          stick
3  ozs. pineapple juice      1 green cocktail cherry
1  oz. lemon juice

Shake gin, crème de menthe, pineapple juice and lemon
juice well with ice. Strain into tall 14-oz. glass. Add a
splash of soda and ice to fill glass. Stir. Garnish with
pineapple stick and cherry.

## PINK LEMONADE A LA PLAYBOY

5  ozs. chilled rosé wine    ½ oz. kirschwasser
2  ozs. chilled lemon         2 teaspoons sugar
    juice                       1 slice lemon
2  ozs. chilled orange        1 maraschino cherry
    juice

Into tall 14-oz. glass, pour wine, lemon juice, orange
juice, kirschwasser and sugar. Stir well until sugar
dissolves. Add two large ice cubes and enough ice-cold
water (not club soda) to fill glass. Stir. Garnish with
lemon slice and cherry.

# PINK RUM AND TONIC

| | |
|---|---|
| 2½ ozs. light rum | Iced tonic water |
| ½ oz. lime juice | 1 slice lime |
| 1 teaspoon grenadine | |

Shake rum, lime juice and grenadine well with ice.
Strain into tall 14-oz. glass half-filled with ice. Add
tonic water. Stir. Add lime slice. Curiously refreshing
yo-ho-ho.

# PLAYBOY COOLER

| | |
|---|---|
| 1¼ ozs. golden Jamaican rum | 2 teaspoons lemon juice |
| 1¼ ozs. Jamaican coffee liqueur | Cola drink |
| 3 ozs. pineapple juice | 1 slice pineapple |

Shake rum, coffee liqueur, pineapple juice and lemon
juice well with ice. Strain into prechilled tall 14-oz.
glass. Add ice to fill glass to 1 inch from top. Add
cola. Garnish with pineapple slice. Serve with long
straw, as at the London Playboy Club.

## QUADRUPLE PINEAPPLE
### (4 single or 2 double drinks)

1   large chilled
    pineapple
½ cup pineapple
    sherbet
6   ozs. light rum

3   ozs. orange juice
1½ ozs. lime juice
½ oz. maraschino
    liqueur

The pineapple should measure at least 7 inches from base to top of fruit, not including stem. Cut a cap off pineapple about ½ inch from top. To remove meat from pineapple, cut a deep circle around edge of pineapple about ½ inch from rim, leaving a large cylinder of fruit which must then be gouged out. A very sharp boning knife is a good instrument for the job. Cut wedges of fruit loose by slicing diagonally toward rim of fruit. Use a grapefruit knife or large parisienne-potato cutter to remove small pieces of fruit. Do not pierce shell of fruit or it will not hold liquid. The cavity of the pineapple should be large enough to hold 2 measuring cups of liquid. Test it for size. Cut hard core of fruit away and discard it. Cut enough tender pineapple meat to make ½ cup fruit in small dice. Into well of blender, put the ½ cup diced pineapple, sherbet, rum, orange juice, lime juice and maraschino liqueur. Blend 5 seconds. Pour into pineapple. Place pineapple in deep dish or bowl surrounded with finely crushed ice. Place two or four colored straws in drink, allowing for two or four pineapple sippers. An elaborate production, beloved by rum barons. A second round may be prepared beforehand from the same pineapple and blended just before refilling pineapple.

## RASPBERRY CLARET CUP

| | |
|---|---|
| 4 ozs. dry red wine | 3/4 oz. raspberry syrup |
| 1 oz. brandy | 1 oz. lemon juice |
| 1 oz. Himbeergeist | Iced club soda |
| (dry white rasp- | 2 or 3 fresh or frozen |
| berry brandy) | whole raspberries |

Be sure wine and brandies are ice-cold before mixing drink. Put three ice cubes into tall 14-oz. collins glass. Pour wine, brandy, Himbeergeist, raspberry syrup and lemon juice into glass. Stir until all ingredients are very well blended. Fill glass with soda. Stir slightly. Float raspberries on top.

## ROCK-AND-RYE COOLER

| | |
|---|---|
| 1½ ozs. vodka | Iced bitter-lemon |
| 1 oz. rock and rye | soda |
| ½ oz. lime juice | 1 slice lime |

Shake vodka, rock and rye and lime juice well with ice. Strain into tall 14-oz. glass half-filled with ice. Add bitter-lemon soda. Stir. Add lime slice.

## ROMAN COOLER

| | |
|---|---|
| 1½ ozs. gin | 1 teaspoon sugar |
| ½ oz. Punt e Mes | Iced club soda |
| ½ oz. lemon juice | Lemon peel |

Shake gin, Punt e Mes, lemon juice and sugar well with ice. Strain into tall 14-oz. glass. Add soda and ice to fill glass. Twist lemon peel above drink and drop into glass.

## ROMAN FRULLATI

3 ozs. gin
¼ cup diced Delicious apple, with skin
¼ cup diced ripe pear, with skin
¼ cup frozen sliced peaches, thawed
1 oz. maraschino liqueur
1 oz. orzata or orgeat
½ cup crushed ice

Put all ingredients into blender. Blend at high speed 20 seconds. Pour into tall 14-oz. glass. Add ice, if necessary, to fill glass to rim.

## RUM AND COCONUT COOLER

2½ ozs. light rum
1 oz. cream of coconut
½ oz. lemon juice
Iced club soda
1 slice lemon
1 maraschino cherry

Shake rum, cream of coconut and lemon juice well with ice. Strain into tall 14-oz. glass half-filled with ice. Add a splash of soda. Garnish with lemon slice and cherry.

## RUM AND PINEAPPLE COOLER

2½ ozs. light rum
2 ozs. pineapple juice
½ oz. lemon juice
1 teaspoon 151-proof rum
1 teaspoon sugar
1 dash Angostura bitters
Iced club soda
1 pineapple chunk
1 papaya chunk in syrup

Shake rum, pineapple juice, lemon juice, 151-proof rum, sugar and bitters well with ice. Strain into tall 14-oz. glass. Add a splash of soda and ice to fill glass. Garnish with pineapple and papaya chunks fastened onto a cocktail spear.

## RUM CITRUS COOLER

| | |
|---|---|
| 2   ozs. light rum | 1   teaspoon sugar |
| 1   oz. orange juice | Iced Seven-Up |
| ½ oz. lime juice | 1   slice lime |
| ½ oz. Cointreau | ½ slice lemon |

Shake rum, orange juice, lime juice, Cointreau and sugar well with ice. Strain into tall 14-oz. glass half-filled with ice. Add Seven-Up. Stir. Garnish with lime and lemon slices. Solace or celebration after 18 holes on the fairway.

## RUM CURAÇAO COOLER

| | |
|---|---|
| 1   oz. dark Jamaican      rum | Iced club soda |
| | 1   slice lime |
| 1   oz. curaçao | ½ slice orange |
| ½ oz. lime juice | |

Shake rum, curaçao and lime juice well with ice. Strain into tall 14-oz. glass. Add a splash of soda and ice to fill glass. Garnish with lime and orange slices.

## RUM ROYALE

| | |
|---|---|
| 1   oz. light rum | 1   dash Peychaud's |
| 2   ozs. sauterne | bitters |
| 1½ ozs. lemon juice | 1   cube pineapple |
| 2   ozs. pineapple juice | 1   maraschino cherry |
| 1   teaspoon sugar | |

Shake rum, sauterne, lemon juice, pineapple juice, sugar and bitters well with ice. Strain into prechilled tall 14-oz. glass. Add ice to fill glass. Affix pineapple cube and cherry to cocktail spear and rest on rim of glass. Created by Al Hawn, head bartender at the Kansas City Playboy Club.

## ST.-CROIX COOLER

| | |
|---|---|
| Peel of ½ large orange | 1 tablespoon brown sugar |
| 2 ozs. light rum | 2½ ozs. orange juice |
| ½ oz. dark Jamaican rum | 1½ ozs. lemon juice |
| 1 oz. brandy | 1 dash orange-flower water |
| | Iced club soda |

Cut orange peel from stem end in one continuing spiral about ½ inch wide. Place peel in tall 14-oz. glass, permitting one end to overhang rim. Shake both kinds of rum, brandy, brown sugar, orange juice, lemon juice and orange-flower water well with ice. Strain into glass. Fill glass to rim with coarsely cracked ice or ice cubes. Add a splash of soda. Stir.

## SAN JUAN SLING

| | |
|---|---|
| ¾ oz. light rum | ½ oz. lime juice |
| ¾ oz. cherry liqueur | Iced club soda |
| ¾ oz. Benedictine | Lime peel |

Shake rum, cherry liqueur, Benedictine and lime juice well with ice. Strain into tall 14-oz. glass half-filled with ice. Add soda. Twist lime peel above drink and drop into glass.

## SCOTCH HORSE'S NECK

| | |
|---|---|
| Peel of whole lemon in one spiral | ½ oz. sweet vermouth |
| 3 ozs. Scotch | ½ oz. dry vermouth |

Place lemon peel in tall 14-oz. glass with one end of peel overhanging rim. Add Scotch and both kinds of vermouth. Fill glass with cracked ice. Stir. Add more ice, if necessary, to fill glass. Every horse's neck is improved if it ages about 10 minutes before sipping.

## SCOTCH SOLACE

2½ ozs. Scotch
½ oz. honey
½ oz. triple sec
4 ozs. milk
1 oz. cream
⅛ teaspoon freshly
    grated orange rind

Pour Scotch, honey and triple sec into 14-oz. glass. Stir until honey is thoroughly blended. Add milk, cream and orange rind. Add ice cubes to fill glass to brim. Stir well. Cold, creamy and soothing.

## SCREWDRIVER WITH SHERRY

½ cup orange juice
2 ozs. oloroso sherry
1 oz. vodka
½ cup crushed ice

Put all ingredients into blender. Blend 20 seconds. Pour into double old-fashioned or tall 14-oz. glass. Add ice cubes to fill glass.

## SINGAPORE GIN SLING

1½ ozs. gin
1 oz. cherry-flavored
    brandy
1 oz. lime juice
  Iced club soda
1 slice lime

Shake gin, cherry-flavored brandy and lime juice well with ice. Strain into tall 14-oz. glass half-filled with ice cubes. Fill glass with soda. Add lime slice.

## SLOE CRANBERRY COOLER

2½ ozs. ice-cold sloe gin
6 ozs. ice-cold cran-
    berry juice
1¼ ozs. lemon juice
1 slice lemon

Pour sloe gin, cranberry juice and lemon juice into tall 14-oz. glass. Add ice cubes to fill glass. Stir well. Add lime slice.

## STEEPLEJACK

2   ozs. apple brandy
2½  ozs. iced apple juice
2½  ozs. iced club soda
1   teaspoon lime juice
1   slice lime

Pour apple brandy, apple juice, soda and lime juice into tall 14-oz. glass. Add ice to fill glass. Stir. Add lime slice.

## STRAWBERRY BLONDE

3   fresh strawberries
1   oz. strawberry
      liqueur
6   ozs. well-chilled
      Rhine wine
½   oz. kirsch
      Iced club soda
1   slice lime

Marinate strawberries in strawberry liqueur for 1 hour. Fasten strawberries onto cocktail spear. Pour Rhine wine, strawberry liqueur and kirsch into tall 14-oz. glass. Add a splash of soda and ice to fill glass. Stir. Add lime slice. Place speared strawberries over rim of glass.

## STRAWBERRY CREAM COOLER

1½  ozs. gin
¼   cup frozen sliced
      strawberries (fruit
      and syrup), thawed
1   oz. lemon juice
2   tablespoons cream
1   teaspoon sugar
      Iced club soda

Put gin, strawberries, lemon juice, cream and sugar into blender. Blend 10–15 seconds at high speed. Pour into tall 14-oz. glass. Add a splash of soda and ice to fill glass. Stir.

# STRAWBERRY VERMOUTH COOLER

2½ ozs. dry vermouth
¼ cup fresh strawber-
ries, hulled and
sliced
1 oz. gin

2 teaspoons red-
currant syrup
½ cup crushed ice
Iced club soda
1 slice lemon

Put vermouth, strawberries, gin, red-currant syrup and ice into blender. Blend 10–15 seconds at low speed. Pour into tall 14-oz. glass containing two ice cubes. Add a splash of soda. Stir. Garnish with lemon slice.

# TALL DUTCH EGGNOG

1½ ozs. advocaat liqueur
1½ ozs. light rum
½ oz. 151-proof rum
1 oz. orange juice
6 ozs. milk

1 teaspoon sugar
½ cup finely cracked
ice
Ground cinnamon

Put advocaat, both kinds of rum, orange juice, milk, sugar and ice into blender. Blend at high speed 10 seconds. Pour into tall 14-oz. glass. Sprinkle with cinnamon. The Dutch way of getting the new year to roll as merrily as possible.

# TALL ISLANDER

2 ozs. light rum
3 ozs. pineapple juice
1 oz. lime juice
1 teaspoon dark
Jamaican rum

1 teaspoon sugar syrup
Iced club soda
1 slice lime

Shake light rum, pineapple juice, lime juice, dark rum and syrup well with ice. Strain into tall 14-oz. glass. Add a splash of soda and ice to fill glass. Stir. Add lime slice. Bound to make natives unrestless.

## TEQUILA SUNRISE

| | |
|---|---|
| 2 ozs. tequila | 1 teaspoon crème de |
| ½ oz. lime juice | cassis |
| ½ oz. curaçao | Iced club soda |
| | 1 slice lime |

Shake tequila, lime juice, curaçao and crème de cassis well with ice. Strain into tall 14-oz. glass half-filled with ice. Fill glass with soda. Stir. Garnish with lime slice. One to contemplate while waiting for the hot chili.

## TIGER TAIL

| | |
|---|---|
| 4 ozs. ice-cold fresh | 1 oz. Pernod |
| orange juice | 1 slice lime |

Pour orange juice and Pernod into tall 12- or 14-oz glass. Add cracked ice to fill glass. Stir. Add lime slice. Magnificent breakfast first course.

## VERMOUTH COOLER

| | |
|---|---|
| 2 ozs. sweet vermouth | 1 teaspoon sugar |
| 1 oz. vodka | Iced club soda |
| ½ oz. lemon juice | 1 slice lemon |

Shake vermouth, vodka, lemon juice and sugar well with ice. Strain into tall 14-oz. glass half-filled with ice. Add soda. Stir. Add lemon slice.

## WATERMELON CASSIS

| | |
|---|---|
| 2 ozs. gin | ¾ oz. lemon juice |
| ½ cup diced water- | ½ cup crushed ice |
| melon, seeds | Iced club soda |
| removed | 1 slice lemon |
| ½ oz. crème de cassis | |

Put gin, watermelon, crème de cassis, lemon juice and

crushed ice into blender. Blend at low speed 10–15 seconds. Pour into tall 14-oz. glass. Let drink settle for a few moments. Add two ice cubes and a splash of soda. Add lemon slice.

## WATERMELON COOLER

½ cup diced water-
    melon, sans seeds
2¼ ozs. light rum
½ oz. lime juice

¼ oz. maraschino
    liqueur
1 teaspoon sugar
½ cup crushed ice
1 slice lime

Put watermelon, rum, lime juice, maraschino liqueur, sugar and ice into blender. Blend 10–15 seconds at low speed. Pour into tall 14-oz. glass. When foam subsides, add ice to fill glass. Stir. Add lime slice.

## WHITE-WINE COOLER

6 ozs. chilled dry white
    wine
½ oz. brandy
2 dashes orange
    bitters
1 teaspoon kümmel
    liqueur

2 teaspoons sugar
½ oz. lemon juice
Iced club soda
Cucumber peel, 2
    inches long, ½
    inch wide

Put wine, brandy, bitters, kümmel, sugar and lemon juice into tall 14-oz. glass. Stir until sugar dissolves. Add a splash of soda and ice to fill glass. Stir. Add cucumber peel.

# Daisies

The daisy, which originated in the mauve decade, is a medium-tall drink served if possible in knob glassware, a silver mug or any vessel that conveys a feeling of sumptuousness. An amalgam of spirits and fruit juice, it is invariably sweetened with a red agent such as grenadine or raspberry syrup and usually topped with a float of some compatible liqueur—a last-minute touch which adds to its subtlety and good humor.

## APPLEJACK DAISY

1½ ozs. applejack
½ oz. lime juice
1 teaspoon raspberry
    syrup
Iced club soda
1 teaspoon ginger-
    flavored brandy
1 slice lime

Shake applejack, lime juice and raspberry syrup well with ice. Strain into tall 8-oz. glass half-filled with ice. Add soda. Stir. Float ginger-flavored brandy on drink. Add lime slice.

## BOURBON DAISY

1½ ozs. bourbon
½ oz. lemon juice
1 teaspoon grenadine
    Iced club soda
1 teaspoon Southern
    Comfort
½ slice orange
1 cocktail pineapple
    stick

Shake bourbon, lemon juice and grenadine well with ice. Strain into tall 8-oz. glass half-filled with ice. Add soda. Stir. Float Southern Comfort on drink. Garnish with orange slice and pineapple stick.

## CANADIAN DAISY

| | |
|---|---|
| 1½  ozs. Canadian whisky | Iced club soda |
| ½  oz. lemon juice | 1  teaspoon Metaxa brandy |
| 1  teaspoon raspberry syrup | 2  fresh or thawed frozen raspberries |

Shake whisky, lemon juice and raspberry syrup well with ice. Strain into tall 8-oz. glass half-filled with ice. Add soda. Stir. Float Metaxa on drink. Add raspberries.

## GIN DAISY

| | |
|---|---|
| 1½  ozs. gin | Iced club soda |
| ½  oz. lemon juice | 1  slice lemon |
| 1½  teaspoons raspberry syrup | 2  sprigs mint |

Shake gin, lemon juice and raspberry syrup well with ice. Strain into tall 8-oz. glass half-filled with ice. Add soda. Garnish with lemon slice and mint sprigs.

## HAWAIIAN DAISY

| | |
|---|---|
| 1½  ozs. light rum | 1  teaspoon 151-proof rum |
| ½  oz. pineapple juice | |
| 1  teaspoon lime juice | 1  papaya chunk in syrup |
| 1  teaspoon grenadine | |
| Iced club soda | |

Shake light rum, pineapple juice, lime juice and grenadine well with ice. Strain into tall 8-oz. glass half-filled with ice. Add soda. Stir. Float 151-proof rum on drink. Add papaya chunk.

# WHISKEY DAISY

| | |
|---|---|
| 1½ ozs. blended whiskey | Iced club soda |
| 1 teaspoon red-currant syrup | 1 teaspoon yellow Chartreuse |
| ½ oz. lemon juice | 1 slice lemon |

Shake whiskey, red-currant syrup and lemon juice well with ice. Strain into tall 8-oz. glass half-filled with ice. Add club soda. Stir. Float Chartreuse on drink. Add lemon slice.

# Fixes

Fixes are medium-tall drinks in which the ingredients are "fixed" in the glass itself, which is packed with crushed or finely cracked ice. As with the cobbler, no club soda or other extender is added, and shaking or straining is unnecessary. The simple fix of liquor, sugar, ice and a slice of lemon is an heirloom from Victorian drinking days. Modern variations make gloriously refreshing summer libations.

## APPLE GINGER FIX

½ teaspoon sugar
1 oz. applejack
1 oz. ginger-flavored
    brandy

½ oz. lemon juice
1 slice lemon

Dissolve sugar in a teaspoon of water in an 8-oz. glass. Add applejack, ginger-flavored brandy and lemon juice. Fill glass with crushed ice. Stir well. Add more ice to fill glass to rim. Stir. Garnish with lemon slice.

## BOURBON SLOE GIN FIX

½ teaspoon sugar
1½ ozs. bourbon
½ oz. sloe gin
½ oz. lemon juice

1 slice lemon
1 slice fresh or bran-
    died peach

Dissolve sugar in a teaspoon of water in an 8-oz. glass. Add bourbon, sloe gin and lemon juice. Fill glass with crushed ice. Stir well. Add more ice to fill glass to rim. Stir. Garnish with lemon and peach slices.

## BRANDY BERRY FIX

| | |
|---|---|
| 1  teaspoon sugar | ½  oz. lemon juice |
| 2  ozs. brandy | 1  slice lemon |
| 1  teaspoon strawberry liqueur | 1  large strawberry |

Dissolve sugar in 2 teaspoons of water in an 8-oz. glass. Add brandy, strawberry liqueur and lemon juice. Fill glass with crushed ice. Stir well. Add more ice to fill glass to rim. Stir. Garnish with lemon slice and strawberry.

## CANADIAN BLACKBERRY FIX

| | |
|---|---|
| ½  teaspoon sugar | ½  oz. lemon juice |
| 1½  ozs. Canadian whisky | 1  slice lemon |
| ½  oz. blackberry liqueur | 1  fresh blackberry, if available |

Dissolve sugar in a teaspoon of water in an 8-oz. glass. Add whisky, blackberry liqueur and lemon juice. Fill glass with crushed ice. Stir well. Add more ice to fill glass to rim. Stir. Garnish with lemon slice and blackberry.

## CHERRY RUM FIX

| | |
|---|---|
| 1  teaspoon sugar | ½  oz. lemon juice |
| 1½  ozs. vodka | 1  slice lemon |
| ½  oz. Cherry Heering or Cherry Karise | 1  brandied cherry |

Dissolve sugar in 2 teaspoons of water in an 8-oz. glass. Add vodka, Cherry Heering and lemon juice. Fill glass with crushed ice. Stir well. Add more ice to fill glass to rim. Stir. Garnish with lemon slice and cherry.

## DERBY RUM FIX

| | |
|---|---|
| 1 teaspoon sugar | 1 slice cocktail orange |
| 2 ozs. light rum | in syrup |
| ½ oz. lime juice | 1 maraschino cherry |
| 1 oz. orange juice | |

Dissolve sugar in 2 teaspoons of water in an 8-oz. glass. Add rum, lime juice and orange juice. Fill glass with crushed ice. Stir well. Add more ice to fill glass to rim. Stir. Garnish with orange slice and cherry.

## GIN MINT FIX

| | |
|---|---|
| 1 teaspoon sugar | 1 teaspoon white |
| 2 ozs. gin | crème de menthe |
| ½ oz. lemon juice | 2 large mint leaves |

Dissolve sugar in 2 teaspoons of water in an 8-oz. glass. Add gin, lemon juice and crème de menthe. Fill glass with crushed ice. Stir well. Add more ice to fill glass to rim. Stir. Tear mint leaves slightly and float on drink.

## IRISH FIX

| | |
|---|---|
| 1 teaspoon sugar | ½ slice orange |
| 2 ozs. Irish whiskey | ½ slice lemon |
| ½ oz. lemon juice | 2 teaspoons Irish Mist |

Dissolve sugar in 2 teaspoons of water in an 8-oz. glass. Add whiskey and lemon juice. Fill glass with crushed ice. Stir well. Add more ice to fill glass to rim. Stir. Garnish with orange and lemon slices. Float Irish Mist on top.

## SCOTCH ORANGE FIX

| | |
|---|---|
| 1　teaspoon sugar | 2　ozs. Scotch |
| 1　3-inch piece orange | ½　oz. lemon juice |
| 　　peel, in one spiral | 1　teaspoon curaçao |

Dissolve sugar in 2 teaspoons of water in an 8-oz. glass. Place orange peel in glass. Add Scotch and lemon juice. Fill glass with crushed ice. Stir well. Add more ice to fill glass to rim. Stir. Float curaçao on drink.

## WHISKEY OUZO FIX

| | |
|---|---|
| 1　teaspoon sugar | 1　teaspoon ouzo |
| 2　ozs. blended whiskey | 　　Lemon peel |
| ½　oz. lemon juice | |

Dissolve sugar in 2 teaspoons of water in an 8-oz. glass. Add whiskey and lemon juice. Fill glass with crushed ice. Stir well. Add more ice to fill glass to rim. Stir. Float ouzo on top of drink. Twist lemon peel above drink and drop into glass.

# Fizzes

Fizzes are effervescent cooling agents all built on lemon or lime juice and iced club soda. They're designed here for tall 14-ounce glasses, but they can easily be stretched into 16-, 18- or 20-ounce portions for further appeasement of parched throats.

## APRICOT ANISE FIZZ

1¾ ozs. gin
½ oz. apricot-flavored
    brandy
¼ oz. anisette
½ oz. lemon juice

Iced club soda
½ brandied or fresh
    apricot
Lemon peel

Shake gin, apricot-flavored brandy, anisette and lemon juice well with ice. Strain into tall 14-oz. glass half-filled with ice. Fill glass with soda. Stir. Add brandied apricot. Twist lemon peel above drink and drop into glass.

## AQUAVIT FIZZ

2½ ozs. aquavit
½ oz. lemon juice
1 teaspoon sugar
½ egg white

1 teaspoon Cherry
    Heering or
    Cherry Karise
Iced club soda
Lemon peel
1 brandied cherry

Shake aquavit, lemon juice, sugar, egg white and Cherry Heering well with ice. Strain into tall 14-oz. glass half-filled with ice. Fill glass with soda. Stir. Twist lemon peel above drink and drop into glass. Add brandied cherry.

## BAYARD FIZZ

| | |
|---|---|
| 2 ozs. gin | Iced club soda |
| ½ oz. lemon juice | 1 slice lemon |
| 2 teaspoons maraschino liqueur | 2 fresh or thawed frozen raspberries |
| 1 teaspoon raspberry syrup | |

Shake gin, lemon juice, maraschino liqueur and raspberry syrup well with ice. Strain into tall 14-oz. glass half-filled with ice. Fill glass with soda. Stir. Add lemon slice and raspberries.

## BLUEBERRY RUM FIZZ

| | |
|---|---|
| 2½ ozs. light rum | Iced club soda |
| 1 teaspoon triple sec | 1 slice lemon |
| ½ oz. blueberry syrup | 3 large fresh blueberries |
| ¾ oz. lemon juice | |

Shake rum, triple sec, blueberry syrup and lemon juice well with ice. Strain into tall 14-oz. glass half-filled with ice. Fill glass with soda. Stir. Add lemon slice and blueberries.

## BRANDIED PEACH FIZZ

| | |
|---|---|
| 2 ozs. brandy | 1 teaspoon banana liqueur |
| ½ oz. peach-flavored brandy | Iced club soda |
| ½ oz. lemon juice | 1 slice fresh or brandied peach |
| 1 teaspoon sugar | |

Shake brandy, peach-flavored brandy, lemon juice, sugar and banana liqueur well with ice. Strain into tall 14-oz. glass half-filled with ice. Fill glass with soda. Stir. Garnish with peach slice.

## BRANDY MINT FIZZ

2 ozs. brandy
2 teaspoons white
   crème de menthe
1 teaspoon crème de
   cacao

½ oz. lemon juice
½ teaspoon sugar
   Iced club soda
2 large fresh mint
   leaves

Shake brandy, crème de menthe, crème de cacao, lemon juice and sugar well with ice. Strain into tall 14-oz. glass half-filled with ice. Fill glass with soda. Stir. Tear mint leaves partially and place on top of drink.

## CALVADOS FIZZ

2 ozs. calvados
½ oz. lemon juice
1 teaspoon sugar
½ egg white

1 teaspoon cream
   Iced club soda
1 slice lime
1 maraschino cherry

Shake calvados, lemon juice, sugar, egg white and cream well with ice. Strain into tall 14-oz. glass half-filled with ice. Fill glass with soda. Stir. Add lime slice and cherry.

## DANISH GIN FIZZ

1½ ozs. gin
½ oz. Cherry Heering
   or Cherry Karise
¼ oz. kirschwasser
½ oz. lime juice

1 teaspoon sugar
   Iced club soda
1 slice lime
1 maraschino cherry

Shake gin, Cherry Heering, kirschwasser, lime juice and sugar well with ice. Strain into tall 14-oz. glass half-filled with ice. Fill glass with soda. Stir. Add lime slice and cherry. A single round will pave the way for a Danish open-sandwich party.

## DUBONNET FIZZ

| | |
|---|---|
| 1 oz. Dubonnet | 1 teaspoon kirschwasser |
| 1 oz. cherry-flavored | Iced club soda |
|    brandy | 1 slice lemon |
| 1 oz. orange juice | 1 fresh or canned |
| ½ oz. lemon juice |    pitted black cherry |

Shake Dubonnet, cherry-flavored brandy, orange juice, lemon juice and kirschwasser well with ice. Strain into tall 14-oz. glass half-filled with ice. Fill glass with soda. Stir. Add lemon slice and cherry.


## FERN GULLY FIZZ

| | |
|---|---|
| 1 oz. dark Jamaican | Iced club soda |
|    rum | 1 slice or chunk fresh |
| 1 oz. light rum |    pineapple |
| 1 oz. pineapple juice | 1 slice lime |
| ¾ oz. lime juice | |

Shake both kinds of rum, pineapple juice and lime juice well with ice. Strain into tall 14-oz. glass half-filled with ice. Fill glass with soda. Stir. Garnish with pineapple and lime slices.


## FRAISE FIZZ

| | |
|---|---|
| 1½ ozs. gin | Iced club soda |
| 1 oz. Chambery fraise | Lemon peel |
| ½ oz. lemon juice | 1 large strawberry, |
| 1 teaspoon sugar |    sliced in half |

Shake gin, Chambery fraise, lemon juice and sugar well with ice. Strain into tall 14-oz. glass half-filled with ice. Fill glass with soda. Stir. Twist lemon peel above drink and drop into glass. Add strawberry. Perfect as an aperitif.

## GIN FIZZ

2   ozs. gin
½   oz. lemon juice
1   teaspoon sugar

Iced club soda
1   slice lemon

Shake gin, lemon juice and sugar well with ice. Strain into tall 14-oz. glass half-filled with ice. Fill glass with soda. Stir. Add lemon slice. Brandy, whiskey, rum or vodka may be used in place of the gin. A 10- or 12-oz. glass may be used instead of the 14-oz., but any diminution in its size only shortens the pleasure of the long, lazy drink implied by a fizz.

## GOLDEN GIN FIZZ

2¼  ozs. gin
1   oz. lemon juice
1   egg yolk
2   teaspoons sugar

Iced club soda
1   slice lemon
Freshly ground nut-
    meg (optional)

Shake gin, lemon juice, egg yolk and sugar well with ice. Strain into tall 14-oz. glass half-filled with ice. Fill glass with soda. Stir. Add lemon slice. Sprinkle with nutmeg if desired.

## JAPANESE FIZZ

2¼  ozs. blended whiskey
¾   oz. port
½   oz. lemon juice
1   teaspoon sugar

Iced club soda
Orange peel
1   cocktail pineapple
    stick

Shake whiskey, port, lemon juice and sugar well with ice. Strain into tall 14-oz. glass half-filled with ice. Fill glass with soda. Stir. Twist orange peel above drink and drop into glass. Add pineapple stick.

## MORNING-GLORY FIZZ

| | |
|---|---|
| 2 ozs. Scotch | 1 dash Peychaud's |
| 1 teaspoon Pernod | bitters |
| ½ oz. lemon juice | Iced club soda |
| 1 teaspoon sugar | 1 slice lemon |
| ½ egg white | |

Shake Scotch, Pernod, lemon juice, sugar, egg white and
bitters well with ice. Strain into tall 14-oz. glass half-
filled with ice. Fill glass with soda. Stir. Add lemon slice.
A drink for the elite of the fizz fraternity.

## NEW ORLEANS GIN FIZZ

| | |
|---|---|
| 2½ ozs. gin | ¼ teaspoon orange- |
| 1 oz. lemon juice | flower water |
| ½ egg white | 2 teaspoons sugar |
| 1 teaspoon cream | Iced club soda |
| | 1 slice lemon |

Shake gin, lemon juice, egg white, cream, orange-flower
water and sugar well with ice. Strain into tall 14-oz.
glass half-filled with ice. Fill glass with soda. Stir.
Garnish with lemon slice. A variation of the Ramos
gin fizz (page 195).

## ORANGE FIZZ

| | |
|---|---|
| 2 ozs. gin | 1 teaspoon sugar |
| 1½ ozs. orange juice | 2 dashes orange bitters |
| ½ oz. lemon juice | Iced club soda |
| 2 teaspoons triple sec | 1 slice orange |

Shake gin, orange juice, lemon juice, triple sec, sugar
and bitters well with ice. Strain into tall 14-oz. glass
half-filled with ice. Fill glass with soda. Stir. Add
orange slice.

## OSTEND FIZZ

| | |
|---|---|
| 1½ ozs. kirschwasser | 1 teaspoon sugar |
| ½ oz. crème de cassis | Iced club soda |
| ½ oz. lemon juice | 1 slice lemon |

Shake kirschwasser, crème de cassis, lemon juice and sugar well with ice. Strain into tall 14-oz. glass half-filled with ice. Fill glass with soda. Stir. Add lemon slice. Splendid with a summer smorgasbord.

## PEACHBLOW FIZZ

| | |
|---|---|
| 2 ozs. gin | 1 teaspoon cream |
| ½ oz. strawberry liqueur | Iced club soda |
| ½ oz. lemon juice | 1 slice lemon |
| ½ teaspoon sugar | 1 large fresh strawberry |

Shake gin, strawberry liqueur, lemon juice, sugar and cream well with ice. Strain into tall 14-oz. glass half-filled with ice. Fill glass with soda. Stir. Garnish with lemon slice and strawberry. A classic old fizz—and a semantic mystery, since there's no peach in the recipe—but a joy for parched throats.

## RAMOS GIN FIZZ

| | |
|---|---|
| 2 ozs. gin | ¼ oz. lime juice |
| 1 egg white | ½ teaspoon orange-flower water |
| ½ oz. cream | 1 cup crushed ice |
| 2 teaspoons sugar | Iced club soda |
| ½ oz. lemon juice | |

Put gin, egg white, cream, sugar, lemon juice, lime juice, orange-flower water and crushed ice into blender. Blend at high speed 5 seconds. Pour into tall 14-oz. glass. Add enough club soda to fill glass. Stir.

## ROYAL GIN FIZZ

| | |
|---|---|
| 2¼ ozs. gin | 2 teaspoons sugar |
| 1 oz. lemon juice | Iced club soda |
| 1 whole egg | 1 slice lemon |

Shake gin, lemon juice, egg and sugar well with ice. Strain into tall 14-oz. glass half-filled with ice. Fill glass with soda. Stir. Add lemon slice.

## RUM COCONUT FIZZ

| | |
|---|---|
| 2¼ ozs. light rum | Iced club soda |
| ½ oz. cream of coconut | 1 slice lime |
| ½ oz. lime juice | |

Shake rum, cream of coconut and lime juice well with ice. Strain into tall 14-oz. glass half-filled with ice. Fill glass with soda. Stir. Add lime slice.

## RUM PINEAPPLE FIZZ

| | |
|---|---|
| 2 ozs. golden rum | ½ oz. lemon juice |
| ½ oz. 151-proof rum | ½ oz. lime juice |
| ⅓ cup fresh pineapple, small dice | ½ cup crushed ice |
| | Iced club soda |
| ½ egg white | 1 slice lime |
| 1 teaspoon sugar | |

Put both kinds of rum, pineapple, egg white, sugar, lemon juice, lime juice and ice into blender. Blend at low speed 10–15 seconds. Pour into tall 14-oz. glass. Add ice cubes to fill glass. Add a splash of soda and lime slice.

## SLOE GIN FIZZ

| | |
|---|---|
| 1 oz. sloe gin (creamy cap) | ¾ oz. lemon juice |
| | Iced club soda |
| 1 oz. gin | 1 slice lemon |

Shake sloe gin, gin and lemon juice well with ice.
Strain into tall 14-oz. glass half-filled with ice. Fill
glass with soda. Stir. Add lemon slice.

## TEQUILA FIZZ

| | |
|---|---|
| 2 ozs. tequila | 1 small egg |
| 1½ ozs. lemon juice | Iced club soda |
| 2 teaspoons sugar | Salt |
| 2 dashes Angostura bitters | |

Shake tequila, lemon juice, sugar, bitters and egg well
with ice. Strain into tall 14-oz. glass half-filled with ice.
Fill glass with soda. Stir. Sprinkle very lightly with salt.

## WHISKEY CURAÇAO FIZZ

| | |
|---|---|
| 2 ozs. blended whiskey | 1 oz. lemon juice |
| ½ oz. curaçao | Iced club soda |
| 1 teaspoon sugar | ½ slice orange |

Shake whiskey, curaçao, sugar and lemon juice well with
ice. Strain into tall 14-oz. glass half-filled with ice. Fill
glass with soda. Stir. Add orange slice.

# Rickeys

The first time you try a rickey, your reaction may be the same kind of shudder you get with the first taste of Campari or Greek olives. But the instant shock of pleasure to a heat-weary body will draw you back until you're happily addicted.

The word *rickey* evokes an immediate association with gin. But the gin rickey—though it's a justifiably renowned classic among warm-weather coolers—is only one among a multitude of these refreshingly effervescent lime libations. Other rickeys can be made by substituting other liquors for gin. Bourbon, blended whiskey, Canadian whisky, Scotch, apple brandy, vodka and rum all make interesting and refreshing rickeys. But more imaginative rickeys may be created, too, as witnessed by these tried and tested formulas.

## APPLE RUM RICKEY

| | |
|---|---|
| ¾ oz. applejack | Iced club soda |
| ¾ oz. light rum | Orange peel |
| ¼ large lime | |

Put three ice cubes into 8-oz. glass. Add applejack and rum. Squeeze lime above drink and drop into glass. Add soda. Stir. Twist orange peel above drink and drop into glass.

## AQUAVIT RICKEY

| | |
|---|---|
| 1½ ozs. aquavit | ¼ large lime |
| 1 teaspoon extra-dry kümmel | Iced club soda |

Put three ice cubes into 8-oz. glass. Add aquavit and kümmel. Squeeze lime above drink and drop into glass. Add soda. Stir.

## FINO RICKEY

¾ oz. very dry (fino)　　¼ large lime
　　sherry　　　　　　　　Iced club soda
¾ oz. gin

Put three ice cubes into 8-oz. glass. Add sherry and
gin. Squeeze lime above drink and drop into glass. Add
soda. Stir. Serve with something salty—such as a bowl
of assorted stuffed olives or anchovy canapés.

## GIN RICKEY

1½ ozs. gin　　　　　　　Iced club soda
½ small lime

Put three ice cubes into 8-oz. glass. Add gin. Squeeze
lime above drink and drop into glass. Add soda. Stir.

## KIRSCH RICKEY

1½ ozs. kirschwasser　　2 large fresh or canned
¼ large lime　　　　　　　pitted black
Iced club soda　　　　　　cherries

Put three ice cubes into 8-oz. glass. Add kirschwasser.
Squeeze lime above drink and drop into glass. Add
soda. Stir. Cut fresh cherries in half, remove pits and
fasten halves onto cocktail spear; or fasten canned
cherries onto spear.

## OUZO COGNAC RICKEY

1 oz. ouzo      ¼ large lime
1 oz. cognac     Iced club soda

Put three ice cubes into 8-oz. glass. Add ouzo and
cognac. Squeeze lime above drink and drop into glass.
Add soda. Stir. Ouzo has a delightful but forceful flavor,
and cognac is one of the few liquors that can stand
up to it and live compatibly with it in the same drinking
glass. A plate of freshly toasted, salted almonds on the
side really brings the ouzo-cognac combination into
proper perspective.

## PEAR RICKEY

1½ ozs. dry pear brandy     Iced club soda
    (Birnebrande)      2 wedge slices fresh
¼ large lime              ripe pear

Put three ice cubes into 8-oz. glass. Add pear brandy.
Squeeze lime above drink and drop into glass. Add
soda. Stir. Fasten the pear slices onto a cocktail spear
and place across rim of glass. Munch pear piecemeal
while you drink.

## PLUM RICKEY

1½ ozs. plum brandy      Iced club soda
    (quetsch, mirabelle   3 wedge slices fresh
    or slivovitz)         ripe plum
¼ large lime

Put three ice cubes into 8-oz. glass. Add plum brandy.
Squeeze lime above drink and drop into glass. Add
soda. Stir. Fasten the plum slices onto a cocktail spear
and place across rim of glass.

## RASPBERRY RICKEY

1½  ozs. Himbeergeist          3   fresh or thawed
 ¼  large lime                         frozen raspberries
     Iced club soda

Put three ice cubes into 8-oz. glass. Add Himbeergeist.
Squeeze lime above drink and drop into glass. Add
soda. Stir. Float frozen raspberries on drink or fasten
fresh raspberries onto cocktail spear as garnish.

## TEQUILA RICKEY

1½  ozs. tequila              Salt
 ¼  large  lime          1   slice cocktail orange
     Iced club soda              in syrup

Put three ice cubes into 8-oz. glass. Add tequila.
Squeeze lime above drink and drop into glass. Add
soda. Stir. Sprinkle lightly with salt. Fasten orange slice
onto cocktail spear. Munch it before or after each
swallow.

# ODDBALLS

# Oddballs

This chapter contains drinks that, like some of those who drink them, refuse to be classified in conventional categories. But each of the offbeat offerings that follow has a special appeal that sets it apart as a perfect potation to please that special someone or to make a fete more festive: the creamy smoothness of a sherry flip sipped next to a blazing fire, the reviving effects of an eye-opening pick-me-up the moanin' after a long night, the nutmeggy goodness of a sweet sangaree, the unparalleled pleasure of the sight and taste of a superbly created pousse-café, the crowning touch that a mist or frappé adds to any dinner. The only thing these drinks have in common—with those we've already discussed as well as with one another—is their excellence as libations for discriminating drinkers.

# Flips

Flips, like pousse-cafés and frappés, prove that good liquids often come in small glasses. A flip is simply a liquor or wine with egg and sugar, shaken to a gay froth. Flips are rich; too much egg makes them over-rich, in fact. For each drink it's best to use a small pullet-size egg or one large egg for two flips. A classic brandy flip, for instance, is made like this: 2 ounces brandy, 1 small egg and 1 teaspoon sugar are shaken with plenty of ice and then strained into a Delmonico glass. The flip is then lightly topped with freshly grated nutmeg. Following the same pattern, standard flips are made by substituting whiskey, gin, rum, applejack, port, sherry or Madeira for the brandy.

The following snug comforts are for winter holidays, mornings after and long, carefree brunches near a glowing fireplace.

## BRANDIED APRICOT FLIP

| | |
|---|---|
| 1½  ozs. brandy | 1   small egg |
| 1   oz. apricot-flavored | 1   teaspoon sugar |
|      brandy |      Grated nutmeg |

Shake brandy, apricot-flavored brandy, egg and sugar well with ice. Strain into prechilled Delmonico glass. Sprinkle with nutmeg.

## COFFEE FLIP

| | |
|---|---|
| 1½  ozs. cognac | 1   teaspoon sugar |
| 1   oz. tawny port |      Grated nutmeg |
| 1   small egg | |

Shake cognac, port, egg and sugar well with ice. Strain into prechilled Delmonico glass. Sprinkle with nutmeg.

## MADEIRA MINT FLIP

| | |
|---|---|
| 1½ ozs. Madeira | 1 small egg |
| 1 oz. chocolate-mint | 1 teaspoon sugar |
| liqueur | Grated nutmeg |

Shake Madeira, liqueur, egg and sugar with ice. Strain into Delmonico glass. Sprinkle with nutmeg.

## PERNOD FLIP

| | |
|---|---|
| 1 oz. Pernod | 1 small egg |
| ½ oz. Cointreau | 1 teaspoon sugar |
| 2 teaspoons lemon juice | Grated nutmeg |

Shake Pernod, Cointreau, lemon juice, egg and sugar well with ice. Strain into prechilled Delmonico glass. Sprinkle with nutmeg.

## STRAWBERRY RUM FLIP

| | |
|---|---|
| 1 oz. strawberry | 1 small egg |
| liqueur | 1 teaspoon sugar |
| 1½ ozs. light rum | Grated nutmeg |
| 1 teaspoon lemon juice | |

Shake strawberry liqueur, rum, lemon juice, egg and sugar well with ice. Strain into prechilled Delmonico glass. Sprinkle with nutmeg.

## STREGA FLIP

| | |
|---|---|
| 1 oz. Strega | 1 small egg |
| 1 oz. brandy | 1 teaspoon sugar |
| ½ oz. orange juice | Grated nutmeg |
| 1 teaspoon lemon juice | |

Shake Strega, brandy, orange juice, lemon juice, egg and sugar well with ice. Strain into prechilled Delmonico glass. Sprinkle with nutmeg.

# TOKAY FLIP

*2½ ozs. imported Tokay*   *1  small egg*
     *wine (Tokaji Aszu)*     *Grated nutmeg*
  *1  teaspoon sugar*

Shake Tokay, sugar and egg well with ice. Strain into
prechilled Delmonico glass. Sprinkle with nutmeg.
It may cause another Hungarian revolution to suggest
that the magnificent imported Tokay be turned into a
flip. Actually the wine turns into sweet bliss.

# Frappes

Frappés and their close cousins, mists, are even more pleasing than ice cream and cake as a finale for a feast. Cool, clean and rich, they're a mixture of liqueurs poured over finely crushed ice. You can serve them freshly made, but we prefer to swizzle them up beforehand and store them in the freezer until the drinking lamp is lit. When you take them out, you'll find that an ice cap has formed on top of each drink. But the cap will loosen after a minute or two and the drink can be sipped from the rim with or without a short straw.

## ALL-WHITE FRAPPE

½ oz. anisette
¼ oz. white crème de menthe
½ oz. white crème de cacao
1 teaspoon lemon juice

Stir without ice. Pour over crushed ice in deep-saucer champagne glass.

## BANANA RUM FRAPPE

½ oz. banana liqueur
½ oz. light rum
½ oz. orange juice

Stir without ice. Pour over crushed ice in deep-saucer champagne glass. Cool postscript for an oriental dinner.

## BRANDY APRICOT FRAPPE

¾ oz. California brandy
¼ oz. crème de noyaux
½ oz. apricot-flavored brandy

Stir without ice. Pour over crushed ice in deep-saucer champagne glass.

## CHARTREUSE COGNAC FRAPPE

¾ oz. yellow Chartreuse    ¾ oz. cognac

Stir without ice. Pour over crushed ice in deep-saucer champagne glass.


## CHERRY GINGER FRAPPE

1  oz. cherry liqueur
¼ oz. kirschwasser
¼ oz. ginger-flavored
    brandy

1  brandied cherry
1  piece preserved
    ginger in syrup

Stir cherry liqueur, kirschwasser and ginger-flavored brandy without ice. Pour over crushed ice in deep-saucer champagne glass. Pierce brandied cherry and preserved ginger with cocktail spear and place over rim of glass.


## CHOCOLATE ORANGE FRAPPE

¾ oz. white crème de
    cacao

¾ oz. orange juice
1  teaspoon Roiano

Stir without ice. Pour over crushed ice in deep-saucer champagne glass. The small amount of vanilla in the Roiano liqueur blends happily with the chocolate in the crème de cacao.


## COFFEE GRAND MARNIER

½ oz. coffee liqueur
½ oz. Grand Marnier

½ oz. orange juice
1  slice orange

Stir coffee liqueur, Grand Marnier and orange juice without ice. Pour over crushed ice in deep-saucer champagne glass. Add orange slice. Sip without straw.

# COGNAC MENTHE FRAPPE

| | |
|---|---|
| *1  oz. green crème de* | *½  oz. cognac* |
| *menthe* | *2  large mint leaves* |

Stir crème de menthe and cognac without ice. Pour over crushed ice in deep-saucer champagne glass. Tear each mint leaf partially and place on drink.

# GRAND MARNIER QUETSCH

| | |
|---|---|
| *1  oz. Grand Marnier* | *¼  oz. orange juice* |
| *¼  oz. quetsch* | *1  slice lemon* |

Stir Grand Marnier, quetsch and orange juice without ice. Pour over crushed ice in deep-saucer champagne glass. Add lemon slice. Mirabelle or slivovitz may be used in place of quetsch, since all are plum brandies. Serve without straw.

# KUMMEL BLACKBERRY FRAPPE

| | |
|---|---|
| *½  oz. kümmel* | *½  oz. blackberry liqueur* |
| *1  teaspoon lemon juice* | *or blackberry-* |
| | *flavored brandy* |

Stir without ice. Pour over crushed ice in deep-saucer champagne glass. Serve with short straw.

# MIXED MOCHA FRAPPE

| | |
|---|---|
| *¾  oz. coffee liqueur* | *¼  oz. crème de cacao* |
| *¼  oz. white crème de* | *¼  oz. triple sec* |
| *menthe* | |

Sugar-frost rim of deep-saucer champagne glass. Fill with crushed ice. Stir liqueurs without ice and pour over ice in glass.

## PERNOD CURAÇAO FRAPPE

½ oz. Pernod  
½ oz. curaçao  
1 teaspoon lemon juice  

2 teaspoons orange juice  
1 thin slice orange  

Stir Pernod, curaçao, lemon juice and orange juice without ice. Pour over crushed ice in deep-saucer champagne glass. Add orange slice.

## SAMBUCA COFFEE FRAPPE

1 oz. sambuca  
½ oz. coffee liqueur  

Roasted coffee beans  

Stir the sambuca and coffee liqueur without ice. Pour over crushed ice in deep-saucer champagne glass. Place the glass on a saucer along with about a half-dozen coffee beans to munch while sipping. It's an Italian custom; the more distinguished the guest, the more coffee beans placed alongside his sambuca.

## SHERRIED CORDIAL MEDOC FRAPPE

1 oz. Cordial Médoc  

½ oz. amontillado sherry  

Stir without ice. Pour over crushed ice in deep-saucer champagne glass.

## SLOE LIME FLAPPE

½ oz. sloe gin  
½ oz. lime liqueur  

½ oz. light rum  
1 slice lime  

Stir sloe gin, lime liqueur and light rum without ice. Pour over crushed ice in deep-saucer champagne glass. Add lime slice. Sip without straw.

# SOUTHERN COMFORT STRAWBERRY FRAPPE

| ¾ oz. Southern Comfort | Orange peel |
| --- | --- |
| ¾ oz. strawberry liqueur | 1 slice lemon |

Stir Southern Comfort and strawberry liqueur without ice. Pour over crushed ice in deep-saucer champagne glass. Twist orange peel above drink and drop into glass. Add lemon slice. Sip on a summer evening under the stars.

# Mists

A mist is simply straight liquor poured over crushed ice. The normal proportions are 1½ ounces of liquor poured into an eight-ounce old-fashioned glass filled with crushed ice. Sometimes a twist of lemon is added. Mists are cousins of frappés, which are sweet liqueurs poured over crushed ice. Actually, the large amount of fine ice in a mist doesn't befog the liquor's intrinsic flavor; the quality of a fine whiskey in a mist will seem more vivid than the same shot bolted straight down. We now draw the veil from ten of the best-known mists.

## BRANDY MIST

The triumphant flavor of cognac makes the noncognac brandies seem pallid by comparison (in mixed drinks the story may be different). Metaxa, the Greek semisweet brandy, creates a velvety, tremulous mist.

## SCOTCH MIST

Best when made with a full-bodied 12-year-old Highland dew. When it comes to mists, some of the lighter Scotches turn into ordinary fog.

## VODKA MIST

Ice and vodka emerge as just ice and vodka, nothing more; but an added dram of dry vermouth (a mere teaspoon or so) and a twist of lemon turn the mist into an instant vodka martini. Zubrovka vodka makes a subtle mist.

## KIRSCHWASSER MIST

A happy, silvery mist with a hauntingly dry aftertaste of cherries.

## BOURBON MIST

Either 86 or 100 proof is fine, but more important than proof is a quality aged bourbon with a smooth, ripe flavor. Half bourbon and half Southern Comfort creates a heavenly mist.

## RYE MIST

One of the best ways of appreciating genuine straight rye.

## BLENDED U.S. WHISKEY MIST

As in bourbon, smoothness shows up in the very first sip. A slice of lemon is a pleasant garnish.

## CANADIAN MIST

Use top Canadian whisky, but increase portion to 1¾ ounces to keep the cool north-country flavor from dissipating too soon.

## GIN MIST

It's surprising how close a gin mist is to the modern martini. Add a tiny splash of dry vermouth for a martini mist. A good way to introduce Dutch genever gin to someone who's never tasted it is via the mist.

## RUM MIST

The potent flavors of Martinique and Jamaican rums emerge beautifully in mists. Light rum is extremely pleasant with a slice of lime or a small gardenia as garnish. For a more rummy accent, float a teaspoon of 151-proof rum on a light-rum mist.

# Pick-Me-Ups

The ancient Egyptians thought that boiled cabbage would prevent a big head after an all-night drinking session. A ground swallow's beak blended with myrrh was recommended by the Assyrians. In South America the Warau Indian women took care of their overindulgent males by deftly tying them like mummies in hammocks until their hangovers passed. In this country the "hair of the dog"—the very thing that caused you to see double—may be the shot in the arm that will straighten your sight. For generations, experienced barmen, especially in men's clubs, where hangover victims can be observed and treated at close range, have vouched for the hair-of-the-dog therapy. Naturally, the danger of taking a swig of liquor the morning after is that the stimulus and relief it brings may provide just enough narcosis to set you right back on the rocky road to ruin. Nevertheless, the effect of a small amount of liquor, especially if combined with citrus juice or tomato juice, seems in many cases to have an extremely salutary effect. The following are from PLAYBOY's repertory of classic and modern pick-me-ups.

## CANADIAN STAVE

| | |
|---|---|
| 2 ozs. Canadian whisky | ¼ teaspoon Angostura |
| 1 oz. Dubonnet | bitters |
| ½ egg white | 2 teaspoons lemon juice |
| | 2 dashes Tabasco sauce |

Shake all ingredients well with ice. Strain into pre-chilled old-fashioned glass. Add ice cubes to fill glass.

# CLAM-JUICE COCKTAIL

| | |
|---|---|
| 4 ozs. clam juice | 1 dash Worcestershire |
| ½ oz. catsup | sauce |
| ¼ oz. lemon juice | Salt and pepper |
| | Celery salt |

Shake clam juice, catsup, lemon juice, Worcestershire sauce, salt and pepper well with ice. Strain into prechilled 6-oz. Delmonico glass. Sprinkle with celery salt.

# COGNAC COUPLING

| | |
|---|---|
| 2 ozs. cognac | 1 teaspoon lemon juice |
| 1 oz. tawny port | ½ teaspoon Peychaud's |
| ½ oz. Pernod | bitters |

Shake well with ice. Strain into prechilled old-fashioned glass. Add ice cubes to fill glass.

# GIN BRACER

| | |
|---|---|
| 2 ozs. gin | 1 dash celery salt |
| ½ oz. catsup | ¼ teaspoon Worcester- |
| ½ oz. lemon juice | shire sauce |
| 1 dash Tabasco sauce | 1 cup crushed ice |

Put all ingredients into blender. Blend at low speed 15–20 seconds. Pour into tall 10-oz. glass. Add ice cubes to fill glass.

# MORNING FIZZ

| | |
|---|---|
| 2 ozs. blended whiskey | 1 teaspoon sugar |
| ½ egg white | ½ teaspoon Pernod |
| ½ oz. lemon juice | Iced club soda |

Shake whiskey, egg white, lemon juice, sugar and Pernod well with ice. Strain into tall 8-oz. glass. Add a splash of soda and ice to fill glass. Stir.

## POLYNESIAN PICK-ME-UP

½ cup pineapple juice
1½ ozs. vodka
½ teaspoon curry
   powder
½ teaspoon lemon juice

1 tablespoon cream
2 dashes Tabasco sauce
½ cup crushed ice
   Cayenne pepper

Put pineapple juice, vodka, curry powder, lemon juice, cream, Tabasco sauce and crushed ice into blender. Blend 10 seconds at high speed. Pour into prechilled old-fashioned glass. Dust very lightly with cayenne.

## PRAIRIE OYSTER

1½ ozs. cognac
2 teaspoons cider
   vinegar
½ oz. Worcestershire
   sauce

1 teaspoon catsup
½ teaspoon Angostura
   bitters
1 egg yolk
   Cayenne pepper

Shake cognac, vinegar, Worcestershire sauce, catsup and bitters well with ice. Strain into prechilled old-fashioned glass. Add an ice cube or two to fill glass almost to rim. Place egg yolk on top of drink without breaking it. Sprinkle yolk lightly with cayenne. This oldest and most stunning of all morning-after drinks should be swallowed in one long, determined gulp. Grit your teeth. Then open your eyes very slowly.

## RUDDY MARY

1½ ozs. aquavit
½ cup tomato juice
1 tablespoon cream
1 dash Tabasco
   sauce

½ egg yolk
¼ oz. lemon juice
¼ oz. catsup
½ cup crushed ice

Put all ingredients into blender. Blend at high speed 20 seconds. Pour into old-fashioned glass. When foam settles, add ice to fill glass to rim.

# Pousse-Cafes

This showy little drink is one of the oldest bits of nonsense known to bartenders—and, needless to say, the number of drinkers who never stop loving nonsense is greater than ever. The pousse-café is a series of liqueurs poured into a small, straight-sided glass so that each forms a layer. Since the liqueurs are of different weights or densities, the heaviest stays on the bottom, the next heaviest directly above it, and so on. The main problem that bedevils the pousse-café specialist is that the densities of liqueurs of the same flavor often vary from one brand to the next. One man's menthe may not rise above another man's parfait amour. Since the density of a liqueur is not indicated on the bottle's label, a certain amount of trial and error may be necessary in building a pousse-café. As a general guide, remember that frequently the higher a liqueur's alcoholic content, the lower its density. This doesn't apply in all cases, but it's something of a help. The so-called *demi-sec* liqueurs are lighter than the sweet crèmes, and U.S. fruit-flavored brandies are lighter than liqueurs. If you're in doubt about a recipe, make an experimental pousse-café before the guests arrive, and when you find a formula that works, stick to it as long as you're using the same brand of liqueurs.

To keep the ingredients from mingling, pour them slowly over the back of a teaspoon, with the tip of the spoon held against the inside of the glass. Pour slowly and steadily, keeping your eye on the liquid as it flows. If you follow this procedure carefully, the layers should stay separate; you may find, in fact, that a liqueur poured in the wrong order will seep down or rise up to its proper level and stay there intact. For a party, you can make a large number of pousse-cafés beforehand, and if you place them carefully in the refrigerator, each small rainbow will remain undisturbed until you need it.

A pousse-café may be of three, four or five layers. Each layer needn't be equal, but each should be of a distinctly different color when held at eye level. Non-alcoholic liquids such as syrups and cream may be poured along with the liqueurs or other spirits.

Here are 11 pousse-café combinations, with the heaviest liquid listed first and the lighter ones in ascending order. To both create and divert conversation, make an assortment with several combinations on the same tray.

White crème de cacao, cherry liqueur, kümmel and a dab of whipped cream.

Green crème de menthe, Galliano, blackberry liqueur and kirschwasser.

Banana liqueur, Cherry Heering or Cherry Karise and cognac.

Peach liqueur, kirsch liqueur (not kirschwasser) and Pernod.

Orzata or orgeat, crème de noyaux, curaçao and sweet cream mixed with enough crème de noyaux to make it pink.

Passion-fruit syrup, green crème de menthe, strawberry liqueur and ouzo.

Grenadine, crème de cacao, Drambuie and sweet cream flavored with crème de menthe.

Crème de noyaux, anisette, Tuaca and a dab of whipped cream.

Grenadine, crème de cacao, triple sec and Forbidden Fruit.

Crème de cacao, maraschino liqueur, Rosémint, yellow Chartreuse and cognac.

Parfait amour, cherry liqueur, anisette and sweet cream flavored with a small amount of parfait amour.

# Sangarees

Sangarees are slightly sweet straight-liquor drinks on the rocks. Unlike an old-fashioned, the sangaree contains no bitters. Each drink receives a benediction of freshly grated nutmeg and should be very well stirred for proper dilution.

## APPLE GINGER SANGAREE

*1½ ozs. apple brandy*          *1  slice lemon*
*½ oz. green ginger wine*        *Freshly grated nutmeg*

Pour apple brandy and ginger wine over rocks in old-fashioned glass. Stir. Add lemon slice. Sprinkle lightly with nutmeg.

## BRANDY SANGAREE

*½ teaspoon sugar*              *1  teaspoon Madeira*
*Iced club soda*                *Orange peel*
*2  ozs. brandy*               *Freshly grated nutmeg*

Stir sugar and 1 tablespoon soda in prechilled old-fashioned glass until sugar dissolves. Add brandy and Maderia. Add ice almost to rim of glass. Stir. Add a splash of soda. Stir. Twist orange peel above drink and drop into glass. Sprinkle lightly with nutmeg.

## GIN BENEDICTINE SANGAREE

*1¼ ozs. gin*                  *1  slice lemon*
*¼ oz. Benedictine*            *Freshly grated nutmeg*
*½ oz. grapefruit juice*

Pour gin, Benedictine and grapefruit juice into prechilled old-fashioned glass. Stir. Add ice to rim of glass. Stir. Add lemon slice. Sprinkle lightly with nutmeg.

## IRISH CANADIAN SANGAREE

1¼ ozs. Canadian whisky    1   teaspoon lemon juice
½ oz. Irish Mist liqueur       Freshly grated nutmeg
1   teaspoon orange juice

Pour whisky, Irish Mist, orange juice and lemon juice
into prechilled old-fashioned glass. Stir. Add ice to rim
of glass. Stir. Sprinkle lightly with nutmeg.

## SANGAREE COMFORT

1   oz. bourbon           1   teaspoon lemon juice
1   oz. Southern Comfort   ½ teaspoon sugar
1   teaspoon peach-       Iced club soda
     flavored brandy      Freshly grated nutmeg

Stir bourbon, Southern Comfort, peach-flavored brandy,
lemon juice and sugar in prechilled old-fashioned
glass. Stir. Add ice to rim of glass. Add splash of soda.
Stir. Sprinkle lightly with nutmeg.

## SCOTCH SANGAREE

½ teaspoon honey      Lemon peel
  Iced club soda       Freshly grated nutmeg
2 ozs. Scotch

Stir honey, 1 tablespoon soda and Scotch in prechilled
old-fashioned glass until honey dissolves. Add ice to
rim of glass. Add a splash of soda. Stir. Twist lemon
peel above drink and drop into glass. Sprinkle lightly
with nutmeg.

# THE BRIMMING BOWL

# The Brimming Bowl

In the world of entertaining, there is no more delight-fully flexible a potable than a good punch. This protean party favorite can assume any festive task to which it's put. Made with light Moselle or Rhenish wines, it can beguile your guests with a light, delicate flavor that rests easily on the tongue. Switch to the heavier-duty brandies and rums and it can singlehandedly catalyze jolly high spirits and flowing conversation.

Nevertheless, for some time the punch bowl was trotted out only at the year-end saturnalia, when it was filled with a hot wassail or a rich whiskey eggnog, emptied a few times and then stashed away in dry storage for the next 12 months. But today, more and more hosts are reviving the reigns of the four Georges of England, when men like David Garrick and Sam Johnson vied with each other all year round to invent newer and stronger punch recipes as they ladled their way through clubs and taverns all over England, and when punch bowls in numerous shapes and sizes sparkled invitingly and were the center of conviviality at celebrations of everything from weddings to military triumphs.

Now, as then, there are a few punch recipes in which fruit has to be marinated in liquors for a day or two, but—happily—those are the exceptions. Generally, an hour or so is all you need for ripening the strong and the weak, the tart and the sweet into a really superior punch. And yet, for all its simplicity, the punch bowl, with its gleaming island of ice in a sea of liquor, turns any casual affair into a gala occasion. The mere sight of the brimming bowl seems an irresistible enticement to drinkers of all persuasions, be they light, moderate or heavy.

Punch is made cold in two ways—by prechilling all the ingredients from the brandy to the bitters, and by placing a floating island of ice in the bowl itself to both cool and properly dilute the liquid—though a few cold punches, such as the champagne varieties, aren't diluted with ice but instead are sometimes ice-girt in a surrounding vessel of crushed ice. These days, when the iceman no longer cometh, it's sometimes difficult to buy a really good-sized chunk. However, in our age of the cube, this is no particular problem; in fact, cubes are faster in their chilling effect than a block. But to serious punch makers, they are puny craft alongside the traditional icy blockbuster in the punch bowl. You can make your own by simply freezing water in a metal or plastic container, a deep saucepan or metal mixing bowl. For each gallon of punch, you'll normally need a chunk of ice made with two quarts of water. After freezing, dip the sides of the bowl in warm water for a few seconds and the ice will slide free. The top may form a slight peak and reveal a crack or two, but the inverted iceberg will be smooth and should float serenely.

The punch recipes that follow each make approximately a gallon of potables, enough for eight bibulous guests at three rounds apiece.

## APPLE GINGER PUNCH

| | | | |
|---|---|---|---|
| 24 | ozs. apple brandy | 24 | ozs. green-ginger wine |
| 2 | ozs. maraschino liqueur | 1 | quart plus 1 pint ginger beer |
| 2 | ozs. kirsch | 2 | red apples |
| 1 | quart pineapple-grapefruit juice | 2 | yellow apples |

Chill all ingredients. Pour all liquids except ginger beer over large block of ice in punch bowl. Stir well. Let mixture ripen 1 hour in refrigerator. Cut unpeeled apples into wedgelike slices. Just before serving, pour ginger beer into bowl. Float apple slices on top.

## ARTILLERYMEN'S PUNCH

| | | | |
|---|---|---|---|
| 1 | quart 86-proof bourbon | 6 | ozs. apricot-flavored brandy |
| 9 | ozs. light rum | 12 | ozs. lemon juice |
| 4 | ozs. dark Jamaican rum | 24 | ozs. orange juice |
| | | 1 | quart strong black tea |
| | | ¼ | cup sugar |

Pour all ingredients over a large block of ice in punch bowl. Stir well. Refrigerate 1 hour before serving.

## BARBADOS BOWL

| | | | |
|---|---|---|---|
| 8 | medium-size ripe bananas | 8 | ozs. 151-proof rum |
| 1 | cup lime juice | 1 | quart plus 12 ozs. pineapple juice |
| 1 | cup sugar | 12 | ozs. mango nectar |
| 1 | fifth light rum | 2 | limes, sliced |

Chill all ingredients except bananas. Cut 6 bananas into thin slices and place in electric blender with lime juice and sugar. Blend until smooth. Pour over block of ice in punch bowl. Add both kinds of rum, pineapple juice and mango nectar. Stir well. Let mixture ripen in refrigerator 1 hour before serving. Cut remaining 2 bananas into thin slices. Float banana and lime slices on punch.

# BERMUDA BOURBON PUNCH

| | |
|---|---|
| 3 tablespoons jasmine tea | 1½ ozs. Pernod |
| 3 cups boiling water | 4 ozs. Falernum |
| 1 fifth bourbon | 1 quart plus 1 pint ginger ale |
| 8 ozs. Madeira | 3 lemons, thinly sliced |
| 8 ozs. lemon juice | |

Pour boiling water over tea leaves. Steep for 5 minutes; strain, cool to room temperature and chill in refrigerator. Over large block of ice in punch bowl pour tea, bourbon, Madeira, lemon juice, Pernod and Falernum. Stir well. Let mixture ripen 1 hour in refrigerator. Add ginger ale and sliced lemons. Add several spiced walnuts (recipe below) to each drink after pouring it into punch cup.

# SPICED WALNUTS

| | |
|---|---|
| 1 egg white | 1 tablespoon ground cinnamon |
| 2 teaspoons cold water | |
| ½ lb. shelled walnuts, halves | ¼ teaspoon ground cloves |
| 1 cup sugar | ⅛ teaspoon ground nutmeg |

Beat egg white until slightly foamy but not stiff. Add water and mix well. Combine egg white and walnuts in a bowl; stir to coat nuts; drain thoroughly in colander to remove excess egg white. In another bowl, combine sugar, cinnamon, cloves and nutmeg. Preheat oven to 325°. Dip walnuts, a few pieces at a time, into sugar mixture (they should be coated thoroughly but should not have thick gobs of sugar adhering to them), place them on a greased baking sheet and bake 20 minutes or until medium brown. Remove from baking sheet with spatula, separating them from sugar coating on pan. Cool to room temperature.

## BLACK-CHERRY RUM PUNCH

| | | | |
|---|---|---|---|
| 1 | fifth light rum | 8 | ozs. fresh lemon juice |
| 4 | ozs. 151-proof rum | 4 | ozs. fresh orange juice |
| 4 | ozs. dark Jamaican rum | 4 | ozs. fresh lime juice |
| 2 | 17-oz. cans pitted black cherries in heavy syrup | 8 | ozs. Cherry Heering |
| | | 8 | ozs. crème de cassis |
| | | 2 | limes, thinly sliced |
| | | 1 | quart club soda |

Put all ingredients except soda into punch bowl. Add block of ice. Stir well. Refrigerate 1 hour. Add soda. Stir well.

## BRANDY EGGNOG BOWL

| | | | |
|---|---|---|---|
| 12 | eggs | 4 | ozs. Jamaican rum |
| ½ | cup sugar | 3 | quarts milk |
| 1 | fifth cognac or non-cognac brandy | 8 | ozs. heavy cream |
| | | | Grated nutmeg |

Carefully separate egg yolks from whites. In punch bowl, combine egg yolks and sugar. Beat well with a wire whisk. Gradually add cognac, rum, milk and cream. Beat well. Taste. Add more sugar if desired. Place the bowl in the refrigerator for at least 2 hours. Just before serving, beat egg whites in a separate bowl or in mixer until stiff. Fold whites into punch. Ladle into cups. Sprinkle with nutmeg.

## CAPE COD CRANBERRY PUNCH

| | | | |
|---|---|---|---|
| 2 | quarts plus 6 ozs. cranberry juice | 1 | teaspoon ground cinnamon |
| 1 | quart 100-proof vodka | ½ | teaspoon ground allspice |
| 6 | ozs. cherry liqueur | ¼ | teaspoon ground nutmeg |
| 1 | tablespoon orange-flower water | 2 | limes, thinly sliced |
| 24 | ozs. orange juice | | |

Chill all liquid ingredients. Mix cinnamon, allspice and nutmeg with a small amount of vodka until a smooth, lump-free paste is formed. Pour the paste and all other liquids over large block of ice in punch bowl. Stir well. Refrigerate 1 hour before serving. Float lime slices on top of punch.

## CHAMPAGNE BLUES

| | |
|---|---|
| 1 fifth blue curaçao | 4 fifths dry champagne |
| 8 ozs. lemon juice | Peel of 2 lemons |

Chill all ingredients. Cut lemon peel into strips 1½ to 2 inches long and ¼ inch wide. Pour curaçao and lemon juice into glass punch bowl. Stir well. Add champagne and stir slightly. Float lemon peel, yellow side up, in bowl. Do not use ice in bowl. It may be surrounded by cracked ice, if desired, by placing glass bowl in vessel of larger diameter.

## CHAMPAGNE PUNCH WITH KIRSCH

| | |
|---|---|
| 4 fifths iced brut champagne | 5 ozs. iced oloroso (cream) sherry |
| 5 ozs. iced kirsch liqueur (not dry kirschwasser) | 4 ozs. iced lemon juice |
| | 16 ozs. iced orange juice |

Pour all ingredients into prechilled punch bowl. Stir lightly. Bowl may be surrounded by ice in larger bowl, or punch may be made in pitchers surrounded by ice.

# CHAMPAGNE PUNCH WITH MARASCHINO

| | |
|---|---|
| 6 ozs. maraschino liqueur | 2 oranges, thinly sliced |
| 6 ozs. cognac | 1 lemon, thinly sliced |
| 1 teaspoon orange bitters | 4 fifths iced brut champagne |

Put maraschino, cognac, orange bitters and sliced fruit into punch bowl. Let mixture brew about 1 hour in refrigerator. Place large chunk of ice in bowl. Pour champagne over ice. Stir slightly.

# CHAMPAGNE SHERBET PUNCH

| | |
|---|---|
| 2 quarts lemon sherbet or lemon ice, frozen very hard | 4 fifths iced brut champagne |
| | 1½ teaspoons Angostura bitters |

Be sure lemon sherbet has been in freezing section of refrigerator set at the coldest point for at least 1 day. Place lemon sherbet in prechilled punch bowl. Pour champagne over sherbet. Add bitters. Stir. Let mixture ripen in refrigerator for 10 minutes before serving.

# FISH HOUSE PUNCH I

| | |
|---|---|
| 1½ cups sugar | 1 fifth golden rum |
| 1 quart cold water (not carbonated water) | 1 fifth Jamaican rum |
| | 24 ozs. lemon juice |
| 1 fifth cognac | 6 ozs. peach-flavored brandy |

Put sugar into punch bowl. Add about 1 cup of the water and stir until sugar is dissolved. Add all other ingredients, including balance of water. Let mixture ripen in refrigerator about 1 hour. Place large chunk of ice in bowl. Ladle punch over ice.

## FISH HOUSE PUNCH II

| | |
|---|---|
| 2 12-oz. pkgs. frozen sliced peaches, thawed | 1 fifth cognac |
| | 1 pint lemon juice |
| | 1 cup sugar |
| 1 quart golden rum | 1 quart ice water |

Put peaches into blender. Blend 1 minute at high speed. Pour over large block of ice in punch bowl. Add rum, cognac, lemon juice, sugar and water. Stir well to dissolve sugar. Refrigerate 1 hour.

## FLORENTINE PUNCH

| | |
|---|---|
| 2 21-oz. bottles coffee-cream Marsala wine | 1 fifth plus 8 ozs. brandy |
| | 4 ozs. lemon juice |
| 2 24-oz. bottles Italian rosé wine | 2 oranges |

Chill all ingredients. Pour both kinds of wine, brandy and lemon juice over large block of ice in punch bowl. Stir well. Refrigerate 1 hour. Cut oranges into thin slices. Cut slices crosswise and float atop punch.

## GIN CASANOVA PUNCH

| | |
|---|---|
| 1 quart gin | ⅓ cup sugar |
| 16 ozs. Casanova liqueur | 1 quart club soda |
| 16 ozs. dry vermouth | 2 lemons, thinly sliced |
| 1 quart unsweetened grapefruit juice | 2 bunches mint |

Chill all ingredients. Pour gin, Casanova liqueur, vermouth and grapefruit juice over large block of ice in punch bowl. Add sugar and stir well. Let mixture ripen 1 hour in refrigerator. Just before serving, add club soda to bowl. Stir. Float lemon slices and mint on punch. (1 cup Strega and 1 cup triple sec may be substituted for the Casanova liqueur.)

# HOT RUM AND RHINE PUNCH BOWL

| | |
|---|---|
| 3 bottles Rhine wine | 4 ozs. maraschino |
| 1 fifth golden rum | liqueur |
| 3 cups orange juice | 6 slices orange, cut in |
| 1½ cups fresh lemon | half |
| juice | 8 ozs. 151-proof rum |
| 4 ozs. orgeat or orzata | |

Cut fresh lemons in half to make lemon juice. Set aside eight empty lemon-shell halves. Put the lemon shells into boiling water and boil for 2 minutes. Remove shells from water. As soon as they are cool enough to handle, press shells gently from end to force peel inside out, making eight cups. Handle gently and do not crack peel. Set aside. In a large pot or saucepan holding at least 6 quarts, heat wine, golden rum, orange juice, lemon juice, orgeat and maraschino liqueur until hot but not boiling. Heating may be done in two batches if necessary. Pour into a silver or pottery punch bowl. Add orange slices. Float lemon cups on punch. Fill each cup with 1 oz. 151-proof rum. Set ablaze. When flames subside, stir to mix contents of lemon cups with other liquids. Pour into punch cups.

## MOSELLE BOWL

| | |
|---|---|
| 1 very ripe medium-size pineapple | 4 24-oz. bottles Moselle wine |
| ½ cup sugar | 1 quart large ripe strawberries |
| 12 ozs. Grand Marnier | |
| 16 ozs. brandy | |

Cut ends off pineapple, remove shell and all "eyes" and cut lengthwise into four pieces. Cut away hard core from each piece; then cut crosswise into thin pieces. Place pineapple, sugar, Grand Marnier and brandy in salad bowl or mixing bowl. Marinate, covered, in refrigerator at least 24 hours. Pour well-chilled wine into punch bowl with large block of ice. Add pineapple mixture and stir well. Let mixture ripen in bowl ½ hour before serving. Cut stems off strawberries. Cut lengthwise in half and float on punch.

## ORANGE ALMOND BOWL

| | |
|---|---|
| 6 ozs. slivered almonds | 1 quart plus 8 ozs. orange juice |
| 2 tablespoons melted butter | 1 teaspoon orange bitters |
| Salt | Peel of 2 large California oranges |
| 18 ozs. blended whiskey | |
| 12 ozs. Danish aquavit | 1½ quarts quinine water |
| 8 ozs. sweet vermouth | |

Preheat oven to 375°. Place almonds in shallow pan or pie plate. Pour butter over almonds, mixing well. Place pan in oven and bake until almonds are medium brown, stirring once during baking. Avoid scorching. Sprinkle with salt. Chill almonds and all other ingredients. Pour whiskey, aquavit, vermouth, orange juice and bitters over large block of ice in punch bowl. Refrigerate mixture for 1 hour. Cut orange peel into narrow strips about 2 inches long. Pour quinine water into bowl. Stir. Float orange peel and almonds on punch.

## PHI BETA BLUEBERRY

| | |
|---|---|
| 1 fifth 100-proof vodka | 2 quarts club soda |
| 16 ozs. Metaxa brandy | 2 lemons, thinly sliced |
| 16 ozs. bottled blueberry syrup | 1 pint cultivated blueberries |
| 12 ozs. lemon juice | |

Chill all ingredients. Pour vodka, Metaxa, blueberry syrup and lemon juice over large block of ice in punch bowl. Let mixture ripen in refrigerator 1 hour before serving. Pour club soda into bowl and stir. Float lemon slices and blueberries on punch.

## WHISKEY PUNCH

| | |
|---|---|
| 3 cups orange juice | 2 quarts blended whiskey |
| 1 cup lemon juice | 1 quart iced club soda |
| 1 cup sugar | |
| 2 lemons, thinly sliced | |

Put fruit juices and sugar into punch bowl. Stir until sugar dissolves. Add lemon slices. Place a large chunk of ice in bowl. Add whiskey. Refrigerate 1 hour. Add club soda. Stir. Additional club soda may be added if desired.

# HOT CHEER

# Hot Cheer

When hot drinks had to wait on icy weather, the ideal accompaniments for a hot-toddy party were a raging blizzard and a roaring fireplace. They're still picturesque backdrops, but nowadays any cool evening in the fall or winter is reason enough for filling the cups to the brim with grogs and nogs—and not just at the hearthside. Almost any casual brisk-weather get-together —a tail-gate party at a football or soccer field, a caravan to the ski country—is perfect for tapping the cordial pleasures of the thermos. And a demitasse cup filled with a blend of warm blackberry liqueur, cognac and lemon is the most tranquil joy we can imagine before sinking into an unbroken night's sleep.

Hot drinks should be just warm enough so that the flavors seem to float like the soft clouds on an old silk painting—but not so hot that they burn the lips. Heat them in a saucepan or chafing dish to just short of the boiling point; then turn off the flame and let them cool somewhat before pouring.

One of the oldest bar tools for making drinks hot was the loggerhead—a long iron tool with a cup or ball at one end. In colonial days the cup was used, among other purposes, for melting pitch to be poured upon the crews of attacking naval vessels; those were the days when men at loggerheads weren't kidding. It's now remembered as a fireplace device for the much more advanced purpose of heating rum flips. In time the loggerhead was succeeded by the poker, which serves just as well for those who feel like indulging in a bit of showmanship. Find one that's ash-free—old pokers with the soot of ages upon them aren't nearly as practical as clean ones that have never seen a fireplace—and heat it glowing hot in a normal gas flame. For reviving drinks that have become coolish from standing too long, keep the poker in the flame for at least three minutes before plunging it into the waiting mug.

The recipes that follow require no such fiery baptism (though it may win applause, it won't improve the drinks); nor are they intended to be enjoyed only at a bibbing party. Just as they can be served day or night, indoors or out, in fair weather or foul, they'll be the best of drinking companions with a colorful variety of meals: a warm Danish toddy of aquavit and Cherry Heering before a smorgasbord or smorrebrod, a buttered bourbon and ginger before a chafing dish of creamed chicken hash, a lime demitasse after an urban luau.

Several of the recipes in this chapter depart from the usual one-drink formula. The reason: For some hot potations the nature of the ingredients makes the preparation of a single drink impractical. The blue blazer, for example, should be prepared for two in order to create a decent blaze. The taste of the gin and jerry becomes unpleasantly eggy unless two are made with each egg. The average *café brûlot* set serves eight, so the *café diable* recipe is for that number. And so on; wherever a recipe makes more than a single drink, it's because careful party and taste testing have shown that the number specified is the minimum for best results. But whichever recipes you try, and for however many people, you'll find that all create warm contentment.

## APRICOT TOM AND JERRY

1 egg, white and yolk
   separated
  Salt
⅛ teaspoon ground
   allspice
⅛ teaspoon ground
   cinnamon
1½ teaspoons sugar

1 oz. apricot-flavored
   brandy
1 oz. blended whiskey
1 oz. milk
1 oz. heavy cream
  Freshly grated
   nutmeg

Beat egg yolk until light. Add a pinch of salt and the allspice, cinnamon and sugar, blending well. Beat white separately in a small, narrow bowl until stiff. Slowly fold yolk into white. Put egg mixture into a 10-oz. tom-and-jerry mug. Heat apricot-flavored brandy, whiskey, milk and cream until bubbles appear around edge of pan. Do not boil. Pour into mug slowly, stirring as liquid mixture is added. Sprinkle with nutmeg.

## BLACKBERRY DEMITASSE

1 oz. blackberry liqueur
   or blackberry-
   flavored brandy
1 tablespoon black-
   berry jelly

½ oz. cognac
½ oz. water
½ teaspoon lemon juice
¼ thin slice lemon

Heat blackberry liqueur, jelly, cognac, water and lemon juice without boiling. Stir well until jelly is completely dissolved. Pour into demitasse cup. Add lemon slice.

## BLUE BLAZER
### (Serves 2)

| | |
|---|---|
| 6  ozs. Irish whiskey or Scotch | ¼  cup boiling water Lemon peel |
| 2  tablespoons honey | |

Both nightcap and toast, the blue blazer should be served steaming hot and sipped slowly. (And to create a decent blaze, it should always be made for two.) For mixing it you need two heavy and rather deep mugs, about 12-oz. capacity. Rinse them with hot or boiling water before mixing the drink. Then pour honey and boiling water into one mug and stir until honey is dissolved. Heat whiskey in a saucepan until it's hot but not boiling. Pour into second mug. Light it. Pour the whiskey—carefully—back and forth between the mugs. The flowing blue-flaming stream will be best appreciated in a dimly lit room. Since a few drams of the blazing whiskey may spill, it's best to pour it above a large silver or china platter. When flames subside, pour the blazer into a thick cut-glass goblet. Twist the lemon peel over the blazer and drop it into the drink. Some bartenders wear asbestos gloves when making a blue blazer.

## BUTTERED APPLE GROG

| | |
|---|---|
| 1  oz. apple brandy | ¼  baked apple, fresh or canned |
| 1  oz. dry vermouth | |
| 2  ozs. apple juice | 1  teaspoon sweet butter |
| 2  whole cloves | 1  slice lemon Sugar |

Heat apple brandy, vermouth, apple juice and cloves until hot but not boiling. Into an old-fashioned glass or coffee cup, put baked apple, butter and lemon slice. Pour apple-brandy mixture into the glass. Add 1 teaspoon syrup if canned baked apple is used, or add sugar to taste. Stir until butter dissolves.

# BUTTERED BOURBON AND GINGER

| | |
|---|---|
| 1½ ozs. bourbon | 1 cinnamon stick |
| 1 oz. ginger-flavored brandy | 6 ozs. apple juice Freshly grated |
| 1 teaspoon sweet butter | nutmeg |

Into a 10-oz. mug or silver tankard, pour bourbon and ginger-flavored brandy. Add butter and cinnamon stick to mug. Heat apple juice up to boiling point, but do not boil. Pour into mug. Stir until butter dissolves. Sprinkle with nutmeg.

# CAFE DIABLE
(8 demitasse cups)

| | |
|---|---|
| 2½ measuring cups extra-strong fresh black coffee | Grated rind of ½ orange |
| | 5 ozs. cognac |
| 2 cinnamon sticks, broken in half | 3 ozs. Grand Marnier |
| 8 whole allspice | 2 ozs. sambuca (anise-flavored Italian liqueur) |
| 4 whole cardamom seeds, removed from shell | 2 tablespoons sugar |

In a deep chafing dish or *café brûlot* set, simmer ½ cup coffee, cinnamon sticks, allspice, cardamom seeds and orange rind about 2 or 3 minutes to release spice flavors, stirring constantly. Add cognac, Grand Marnier and sambuca. When liquors are hot, set ablaze. Stir with a long-handled ladle or spoon until flames subside. Add balance of coffee and sugar. When *café diable* is hot, ladle or spoon it into demitasse cups. A delightful postprandial drink—but you'd best rehearse it before debuting for guests. Once learned, it's an amiably engaging routine.

## CREME DE CACAO NIGHTCAP
### (Serves 4)

| | |
|---|---|
| ¼ cup heavy sweet cream | 10 ozs. milk |
| 2 teaspoons sugar | 4 ozs. crème de cacao |
| 1 tablespoon crème de cacao | 2 ozs. California brandy |
| | 3 tablespoons sugar |
| | Cocoa |

Beat cream in small, narrow bowl until whipped. Stir 2 teaspoons sugar and 1 tablespoon crème de cacao into whipped cream. Store in refrigerator until needed. Heat milk, 4 ozs. crème de cacao, brandy and 3 tablespoons sugar until hot but not boiling. Pour hot milk mixture into four footed whiskey-sour glasses or small goblets. Spoon whipped cream on top. Put a small quantity of cocoa into a small fine wire strainer. Shake strainer above each drink, sprinkling lightly with cocoa. Place glass on saucer for serving.

## DANISH TODDY

| | |
|---|---|
| 2 whole cloves | 2 ozs. Cherry Heering or domestic Cherry Karise |
| 2 whole allspice | |
| 1 cinnamon stick | |
| 1 slice orange | 1 oz. aquavit |
| | ½ oz. kümmel liqueur |
| | 5 ozs. cranberry juice |

Put cloves, allspice, cinnamon stick and orange slice into a 10-oz. mug. Heat Cherry Heering, aquavit, kümmel and cranberry juice until hot but not boiling. Pour into mug.

## GIN AND JERRY
### (Serves 2)

| | |
|---|---|
| 4 ozs. gin | 1 teaspoon sugar |
| 1 oz. yellow Chartreuse | 1 egg |
| 3 ozs. orange juice | Ground cinnamon |

Pour gin, Chartreuse, orange juice and sugar into saucepan. Heat almost to boiling point, but don't boil. Beat egg in narrow bowl with rotary beater until egg is very light and foamy. Slowly, while stirring constantly, pour hot liquid into bowl. Pour into preheated tom-and-jerry mugs or punch cups. Sprinkle lightly with cinnamon.

## HOT BUTTERED RUM

| | |
|---|---|
| 2 whole cloves | ½ oz. hot dark |
| 2 whole allspice | Jamaican rum |
| 1 inch stick cinnamon | Boiling water |
| 1 teaspoon sugar | 1 teaspoon sweet butter |
| 1½ ozs. hot light rum | |

Put the cloves, allspice, stick cinnamon and sugar into a mug with a tablespoon or two of boiling water. Let the mixture stand 5 minutes. Add the hot rum (both kinds), 2 ozs. boiling water and butter. Stir until butter dissolves. Add more sugar if desired.

# PLAYBOY'S HOT BUTTERED RUM

| | |
|---|---|
| 2 ozs. dark Jamaican rum | 1 pat butter, equal to 2 teaspoons |
| ½ teaspoon maraschino liqueur | Boiling water |
| 1 oz. lemon juice | 1 slice lemon |
| 1 teaspoon sugar | Freshly grated nutmeg |

Pour rum, maraschino liqueur and lemon juice into 12-oz. mug. Add sugar and butter. Fill with boiling water. Stir to dissolve butter and sugar. Add lemon slice. Grate nutmeg on top. As served at the Lake Geneva Playboy Club-Hotel.

# HOT DRAMBUIE TODDY

| | |
|---|---|
| 2 ozs. Drambuie | 1 slice orange |
| ½ oz. lemon juice | 4 ozs. boiling water |
| 1 slice lemon | 1 piece stick cinnamon |

Pour Drambuie and lemon juice into preheated mug or punch cup. (To preheat mug, fill with boiling water for about a minute; then discard water.) Add lemon slice, orange slice and 4 ozs. boiling water. Stir with cinnamon stick—and leave it in the mug.

# HOT EGGNOG

| | |
|---|---|
| 1 egg | 2 ozs. hot cognac |
| Salt | 1 teaspoon dark Jamaican rum |
| 1 tablespoon sugar | |
| ¾ cup (6 ozs.) hot milk | Ground nutmeg |

Put whole egg and dash of salt into mixing bowl. Beat egg until it is very thick and lemon yellow in color. Add sugar and beat until sugar is blended in. Add hot milk, cognac and rum. Stir well. Pour into mug. Sprinkle lightly with a dash of ground nutmeg.

## HOT PORT FLIP

| | |
|---|---|
| 3 ozs. port wine | 1 small egg |
| 1 oz. cognac | 1 tablespoon heavy |
| 1 teaspoon sugar | cream |
| ¼ teaspoon instant | Freshly grated |
| coffee | nutmeg |

Pour wine and cognac into saucepan. Add sugar. Stir well. Heat but don't boil. Stir in instant coffee. In a narrow bowl, beat egg with rotary beater until egg is very foamy. Stir in cream. Very slowly, while stirring constantly, pour hot liquid into egg mixture. Pour into preheated mug. Sprinkle with nutmeg.

## HOT TODDY

| | |
|---|---|
| 1 teaspoon sugar | 2 ozs. hot bourbon |
| 3 whole cloves | 2 ozs. boiling water |
| 1 inch stick cinnamon | Ground nutmeg |
| 1 thin slice lemon | |

Into a heavy mug, put the sugar, cloves, stick cinnamon and slice of lemon. Add 2 tablespoons boiling water. Stir well. Let the mixture stand about 5 minutes. Add the hot bourbon and the 2 ozs. boiling water. Stir. Sprinkle lightly with nutmeg.

## IRISH COFFEE

| | |
|---|---|
| 5 to 6 ozs. fresh, hot | 1 teaspoon sugar |
| black coffee | Sweetened whipped |
| 1½ ozs. Irish whiskey | cream |

Warm an 8-oz. goblet by rinsing it in very hot or boiling water. Pour coffee and whiskey into goblet. Add sugar. Stir until sugar is dissolved. Add a generous dab of whipped cream.

## LIME DEMITASSE

1 oz. lime liqueur
½ oz. light rum
½ oz. pineapple juice

½ teaspoon fresh lime
  juice
½ oz. water
Lime peel

Heat lime liqueur, rum, pineapple juice, lime juice and water until hot but not boiling. Pour into demitasse cup. Twist a piece of lime peel above drink and drop into cup.

## MEXICAN COFFEE

1 oz. Mexican coffee
  liqueur
4 ozs. fresh, hot black
  coffee

Ground cinnamon
Sweetened whipped
  cream

Pour liqueur into Irish-coffee glass. Pour enough coffee to fill glass to ½ inch from top. Sprinkle with cinnamon. Stir. Top with whipped cream. As served in the Chicago Playboy Club.

## MULLED CLARET
(6 to 8 drinks)

1 cup boiling water
½ cup sugar
1 lemon, sliced
1 orange, sliced

12 whole allspice
12 whole cloves
4 inches stick cinnamon
1 fifth dry red wine

In a large saucepan, combine the boiling water, sugar, sliced lemon, sliced orange, allspice, cloves and stick cinnamon. Bring to a boil. Reduce flame and simmer 5 minutes. Add the wine. Bring up to the boiling point. Do not boil, but simmer 10 minutes. Pour the hot mulled wine into glasses or mugs. Place a slice of lemon, a slice of orange and a few whole spices in each glass.

## MULLED MADEIRA AND BOURBON

2½ ozs. Madeira
1 oz. bourbon
1 oz. Lillet
1 teaspoon orange
    bitters
4 ozs. water
1 tablespoon brown
    sugar
1 cinnamon stick
2 whole cloves
½ slice lemon
Orange peel

Heat Madeira, bourbon, Lillet, orange bitters, water and brown sugar until hot but not boiling. Put cinnamon stick, cloves and lemon slice into 10-oz. mug or metal tankard. Fill mug with Madeira mixture. Twist orange peel above drink and drop into mug.

## MULLED SCOTCH

2 ozs. hot Scotch
1 oz. hot Drambuie
2 dashes bitters
1 oz. boiling water
1 maraschino cherry
Lemon peel

Into an old-fashioned glass, pour the Scotch, Drambuie, bitters and boiling water. Stir. Add the cherry. Twist lemon peel above the drink; then discard the peel.

## MULLED SCOTCH AND GRAPEFRUIT

2 ozs. Scotch
1 oz. Forbidden Fruit
    liqueur
2 ozs. orange juice
2 ozs. grapefruit juice
2 teaspoons honey
1 slice orange
2 whole cloves
1 cinnamon stick

In a saucepan, heat Scotch, Forbidden Fruit, orange juice, grapefruit juice and honey up to boiling point, but don't boil. Stir well to dissolve honey. Press cloves into flesh of orange slice. Pour hot liquid into preheated mug. Float orange slice on drink. Place cinnamon stick in mug. Drink improves after a minute as the aroma of spices gradually ripens.

# ROCK-AND-RYE TODDY

| | |
|---|---|
| 2  ozs. rock and rye | 3  ozs. boiling water |
| 2  dashes Angostura | 1  cinnamon stick |
|      bitters |      Grated nutmeg |
| 1  slice lemon | |

Pour rock and rye and bitters into old-fashioned glass.
Add lemon slice. Add boiling water and cinnamon
stick. Stir. Sprinkle with grated nutmeg.

# SHERRIED SCOTCH

| | |
|---|---|
| 1½ ozs. Scotch | 1  oz. orange juice |
| 1½ ozs. oloroso or cream | 1  dash Angostura |
|      sherry |      bitters |
| 1  teaspoon heather | 1  cinnamon stick |
|      honey | 1  slice orange |

Heat Scotch, sherry, honey and orange juice until very
hot but not boiling. Stir well to dissolve honey. Add
bitters. Pour into old-fashioned glass or glass punch
cup. Add cinnamon stick and orange slice. Stir.

# SOUTHERN BLAZER
(Serves 2)

| | |
|---|---|
| 1½ ozs. Southern | 1½ ozs. coffee liqueur |
|      Comfort | 2  pieces lemon peel |
| 2  dashes Angostura | 2  pieces orange peel |
|      bitters | 3  ozs. boiling water |

Heat Southern Comfort, bitters and coffee liqueur until
hot but not boiling. Pour into one 10-oz. mug. Pour
boiling water into a second mug. Set mug with liquors
ablaze. Pour into mug with boiling water, and immediately pour liquids back and forth until the blazing
stream subsides. Divide mixture between the two mugs.
Twist a piece of lemon peel and a piece of orange peel
above each drink and drop into mugs.

## SWEDISH GLOGG
### (Serves 6 to 8)

| | |
|---|---|
| 1 fifth dry red wine | 1 cup brandy |
| ½ cup sugar | Raisins |
| 16 whole cloves | Peeled unsalted |
| 8 2-inch pieces stick cinnamon | almonds |

In a large saucepan, combine the wine, sugar, cloves and stick cinnamon. Bring to the boiling point. Reduce flame and simmer 5 to 8 minutes. Stir in the brandy. Put a few raisins and almonds into each mug or glass. Add the glogg and serve.

## TOM AND JERRY
### (Serves 8)

| | |
|---|---|
| 2 large eggs | ¼ teaspoon ground cloves |
| ¼ cup sugar | |
| 2 ozs. dark Jamaican rum | 1 pint hot blended whiskey or hot bourbon |
| ½ teaspoon ground cinnamon | 1 quart hot milk |

Most tom-and-jerry recipes call for separating the egg yolks from the whites and beating each separately. If you have an electric blender, however, you can beat the whole eggs and get a fine foamy mixture. You can get the same results if you have a good manual eggbeater and enough muscle power. In any case, beat the whole eggs until they're just beginning to get stiff; then slowly add the sugar. Continue beating until the mixture is very stiff and light lemon yellow in color. Add the rum, cinnamon and cloves. Beat a moment more to blend spices. Spoon the batter into tom-and-jerry mugs. Add 2 ozs. of blended whiskey or bourbon to each mug. Fill the mug with hot milk and serve.

# INDEX

# Index

# MORE FOOD AND DRINK
## FROM PLAYBOY PRESS

**PLAYBOY'S GOURMET**                    $1.25
THOMAS MARIO
Everything you need to know to establish your reputation
as the perfect host and chef.


**PLAYBOY'S BOOK OF PARTIES**            $1.25
THOMAS MARIO
Parties for two, four or fifty.


**THE COOL APPROACH**                    $1.50
THOMAS MARIO
Nearly 400 food and drink recipes for the summer host.


**PLAYBOY'S INTERNATIONAL GOURMET**   $1.25
THOMAS MARIO
Foreign fare for dinner.


**PLAYBOY'S PARTY DRINKS**               $1.25
Everything you need to know to create festive drinks ap-
propriate for winter, for summer, for all seasons of the year.


**PLAYBOY'S WINE GUIDE**                 $1.50
The ABCs of selecting, storing and serving wine.